PROVIDENCE

A STORY OF HOPE, LOVE AND DIVERSITY

SHAWN HALL AND JOYCE HALL

PROVIDENCE

A STORY OF HOPE, LOVE AND DIVERSITY

Written by Shawn Hall and Joyce Hall

Edited by Angela Overby
Designed by Wendy Byle, Byle Design and Associates

Published by

ACORN PRESS

Printed in the United States

ALSO BY JOYCE HALL
KNOWN AS JOYCE BENNETT

ABCs of Your Success
www.ABCsof Living.com

DEDICATION

<u>*IN MEMORY OF*</u>

James Ray Hall

Mark Jason Hall

Terry Jo Hall

<u>*DEDICATED TO*</u>

Chris Hall

Dawn Hall

Denise Hall

Errica Hall

James Ray Hall, Jr.

Jozelle Hall

Michelle Hall

Navia Hall

Ray Hall

Tonda Hall

Tricia Hall

Yvette Hall

Robert Barango

Julie Tunnermann

Mr. & Mrs. Pennington

Mr. & Mrs. Lofton

This book is also dedicated to our friends and family members who have supported us on our journey, and those who suffer from a mental illness, PTSD and/or addiction and their families.

AUTHOR'S NOTES

THOSE EYES, SUCH BEAUTIFUL EYES. Eyes that were telling a story, a story that had me intrigued. They seemed to pull me in. I was getting lost in them. I was aware of people talking, however, didn't really hear any of the words. When I finally was able to find my way back, I heard him say, my name is Shawn. I didn't know then, but I was in for a journey, a journey that would reveal the story those eyes were trying to tell. I knew that this relationship was going to be something special, for it already was.

I met Shawn in a locked medical facility in Pomona, California. Our relationship developed over the next ten years. It became deeper, as time went on. Shawn wanted his life story written down to share with others in hopes it can help someone to make better choices in their lives and never give up hope. He is hoping his story will inspire others to never give up hope no matter where they came from or what circumstances they find themselves in.

I also wanted this story told, as I became part of it. My inspiration is that no matter how old you are, sometimes the best is saved for last. Although, my life has always been fulfilling there seemed to be something missing. No matter how many people came in and out of my life, no matter where I traveled, there was always something missing. In some ways life is like a puzzle. As we go through life, we pick up puzzle pieces represented by people, places, and experiences creating our own unique expression of life through our puzzle. Sometimes we have trouble finding a piece to fit into our existing picture. That's when we spend too much time searching and searching for just the right piece, when all we have to do is just keep living life and somehow, mysteriously that piece shows up. The ultimate meaning of faith.

PROLOGUE

SHAWN, A YOUNG MAN with a mental illness, possibly due to the adversities, abuse, neglect along with a parental death during his young life meets Joyce, a loving, caring older woman who loves her life but always felt as something was missing. She has loved, been married, has two children, developed a good career, traveled, yet, something was missing. She couldn't put her finger on it; she just knew something was missing. This story is about these two people and their very unlikely love affair. Two people coming from two different worlds. Their individual journeys, each on their own quest. One being freedom, safety, security and love. The other searching for an accepting, loving life partner. Each finding that missing piece to complete their life's puzzle. Together they continue their life as one by creating a new life puzzle, once piece at a time.

As you read *Providence* you'll get to know Shawn and Joyce on many levels. It can be read as a metaphor for your own journey. As you put together your life's puzzle, ask yourself, "Are any pieces missing?" If so, maybe, just maybe Shawn and Joyce can be an inspiration in finding them.

CHAPTER ONE

THERE I WAS AGAIN, in my shorts, handcuffed and heading toward the back seat of a squad car. As I was kicking, spitting and acting like a fool, my head was being pushed down as I plopped onto the rear seat. My head was swirling, and I was having trouble clearing my thoughts. What the hell was going on? I knew that I had been in a fight at the board and care facility, however that was not an unusual occurrence. After my part in the fight, I went back to my room and collapsed.

With lights twirling and sirens blasting, the police pulled up in front of our building. The next thing I knew I was being pulled out of my room. Now, here I sit, in the back seat of a squad car, a much too familiar place. Someone was apparently hit over the head with a bottle and got cut during the fight. Even though I had been drinking, I knew that I had not hit anyone with a bottle. I was part of the fight, but there was always some kind of fight going on. The guy that got hit was crazy. He used to walk around with a hammer just ready to hit someone in the head with it. I always had to be on my guard, since I was one of his main targets. So, I'm glad that someone got him first.

We drove all the way to the county jail. Because I was drunk and angry I wouldn't let the police take my fingerprints, so I couldn't stay. So they had to drive me all the way back to the local police station, which really pissed them off. They really hated on me. After sleeping all night in a holding cell I sobered up, ate some breakfast, and we were off once again to the county jail. This time, I let them take my fingerprints and I was escorted to a cell.

"All rise for Judge blah blah." Court proceedings were a joke. My public defender actually got me a DA reject which basically means that the charge was thrown out. Being railroaded in court is not new, and I was now another victim of the justice system. Sentenced to prison for six years for assault and robbery, I was so confused. Of course, part of that confusion came from being off my medication. However, I was clear enough to realize that I was now going to prison for something I did not do. It actually turned out to be the best break I ever received.

I almost did not make it my first year. I acted out, was restrained by the guards, hung myself, and experienced what hell must be like. In what is called five-point restraint, straps are placed in such a way that I could not move. I realized that I had taken life and freedom for granted. Off my medication for a couple of days, my behavior became wild, violent, and scary. To protect themselves, the guards put me in a cage that was about 4' by 7' where I had to stand the entire time I was in there. Reality was blurred by delusions and my delusions became my reality.

Reception, where prisoners are held before being sent to their designated prison, is where I found myself. Voices in my head were saying "you are going to die, you're time is up on earth, you're worthless, you are gonna die, you going to be stabbed." Paranoia was running rampant in me. My cell mate tried to help me, however, I just ended up crying.

I became very verbal to the guards, started to act out, and just plain acted like the fool. Of course, being out of my medication just amplified my behavior. Guards tried to get me out of the cell. Of course, I did not cooperate. In prison, they do have a way of getting your cooperation. Handcuffed, I was placed in a cage. I just became much more verbal, loud swearing, and yelling at the guards and anyone who could hear me. Socking the cage became my recreation, although the consequences of that was a very badly swollen hand.

With a swollen hand, and a sore, scratchy throat, I was back in a cell. After that cage, I was so full of anger that I bit my lip, drew blood, and proceeded to write on the wall "THUG LIFE." A rapper used to use this in one of his songs and it always stayed with me. I could relate to it on so many levels. "The Hate U Gave Little Infants Every Day." I also wrote

"B1" but did not know what that meant, so I erased it. Later the why became apparent. I also used the blood to write "Bible" which meant to me, "Believe In Being Loved Every day." Of course, the guards didn't appreciate my artwork.

My artwork cost me seven days in what is called five-point. Wearing nothing but a smock and a pamper, I spent the next seven days lying on a bed that was on the floor, strapped down in a five-point position. My legs were in so much pain, and I needed to stretch them. I was not allowed to move. Finally, a nurse came. Instead of letting me stretch my legs, she said she was giving me something for pain. However, she didn't. She gave me an anti-psychotic drug so she did not have to mess with me. They call this "booty juice." Now I was not only strapped down, in pain, thirsty, and lying in a pee-soaked pamper, I was drugged up. "What was happening to me?" What a horrific experience!

Snoring, heavy breathing all around me, fire falling from the sky, and voices telling me that people were digging a hole to put me in. I was tripping! I felt pressure on my chest. I saw myself in an arena fighting like a gladiator; only I was a gladiator that was losing the battle. Somehow I had lost my shield in battle and now I was being squashed by my opponent. Shields are supposed to protect, not squash. I came back to reality when I realized I was being squashed under the weight of a guard's shield, not a gladiator's. Although, I am sure that some guards feel like they are doing battle in an arena like gladiators.

I heard myself say, "Okay, okay, I will calm down." What choice do I have if I don't want to be hurt? When my food came in, one of my arms was freed so I could feed myself. However, the voices told me my food was poisoned, so I only drank the juices. Boy, I was sure hungry!

Since I seemed to have settled down, the guards allowed me to return to my cell. Back in my cell, I peered out the window that overlooked a guard's desk. I noticed a woman was reading the newspaper. I looked down at what she was reading and saw **B1**, which was a column with the heading, *"Mother won't take charge of infant son."* I freaked out as I realized somehow I knew that. I had written **B1** on the wall and didn't know why. Now I knew.

I heard someone say, "He knew this." I didn't understand how I knew, became scared and let my behavior, once again, become out of control. Of

7

course not without recourse, with mace in my eyes, I heard myself scream, "Take me to the showers."

There I was back on the floor, strapped down, and back in pampers. This is not the way life should be. My medication finally came. Oh, thank God! However, in the beginning I spit it out every time it was given me. I still didn't trust, yet I knew I was out of control without it. I began swallowing my medication, started to come around, and become a little clearer.

A white guy wearing a hat, the one with the kangaroo in a sitting position on it, came in and introduced himself as a doctor. I commented on his hat and he asked me what the kangaroo meant to me. I told him that it meant "not hopping away from your problems." He gave me a high five and I knew that we were going to get along. The first nice person I've met on this leg of my journey. Hopefully, there are more.

CHAPTER TWO

MOMENTS TO REMEMBER

H OW BEAUTIFUL THE SUN'S REFLECTION is on the water. Having my morning coffee overlooking the ocean from the deck of a ship is what I call "living the life." The water looks smooth as glass, yet I can feel the rocking of the ship. Even though I am in the middle of the ocean, with no land in sight, the rocking gives me such a soothing, secure feeling. I needed that feeling this morning, as I have been feeling a little disconnected lately.

When my husband, Don, suggested that we take a cruise somewhere in the Caribbean, I jumped at the chance. I knew we would have to board the ship in Florida, where my dad lived. I hadn't seen my dad for a couple of years. So, I flew in a couple of days before Don so I could spend some time alone with dad. I knew his wife would give us some space.

It felt so good to spend some quality time with my dad this week. Living so far away from each other is difficult at times, although, the weekly telephone calls help. We talked about his time in World War II as a turret gunner in a B24 Liberator bomber. How he really hated to fly, but there he was, up in the air in a plane, and dodging shrapnel from the bursting bombs below. Like so many young men in his day, he joined the military during the war. Once he was assigned as a turret gunner, he realized that it wasn't all it was cracked up to be. To get out of the service quicker,

My dad and me.

he signed up for extra bombing missions. He never really thought about why there were so many openings for turret gunners. Of course, if he had, he would have realized that sitting on top of a plane with a gun makes for a good target. Many gunners were killed during their missions. So squads would post for gunners. Needless to say, he flew his missions, plus the extra ones, until he reached thirty-three; the minimum to be discharged. He hasn't flown since the end of that war. He actually had a copy of the missions that he flew. It was now in my possession. Along with his leather bomber jacket that once had 33 gold bombs on it, one for each mission, and a picture of a plane that was obviously drawn by a sharp instrument of some sort. The word *Scrooch* was also etched on the jacket, under the picture of the plane. Time has worn the gold off, leaving only a shadow of each bomb in its place.

We reminisced about our time in Augusta, Georgia, where he was stationed when he was called back into the service to train troops for the Korean conflict. I used to love to go to the base and playing on the tanks, shopping at the Post Exchange and watching the troops march in cadence.

```
                    764 Bombardment Squadron (H)
                    Office of the Operations Officer
                    APO 520                    US Army
                                               August 7, 1944

                              Certificate

        I certify that Robert (NMI) Arndt 16144058, has completed
     the following missions, with dates, times, and targets listed below.

     Date              Time              Targets
     April 3, 1944     4:40 hrs.         Drnis, Yugoslavia
       "    6,   "     6:00  "           Zagreb,     "
       "    7,   "     Abort             Ferrara, Italy
       "   10,   "     5:40 Hrs.         Zagreb, Yugoslavia
       "   15,   "     7:00  "           Bucharest, Rumania
       "   16,   "     6:30  "           Brasov,  Rumania
       "   20,   "     6:30  "           Ferrara, Italy
       "   23,   "     7:45  "           Voslau, Austria
       "   30,   "     7:10  "           Alessandria, Italy
     May    2, 1944    7:30 Hrs.         Parma, Italy
       "    5,   "     8:00  "           Ploesti, Rumania
       "    7,   "     8:00  "           Bucharest,  "
       "   12,   "     7:00  "           Viareggio, Italy
       "   14,   "     6:00  "           Padova, Italy
       "   18,   "     6:00  "           Belgrade, Yugoslavia
       "   22,   "     6:45  "           Piombino, Italy
       "   24,   "     7:45  "           Wiener-Neustadt, Austria
       "   25,   "     6:30  "           Carnoules, France
       "   27,   "     8:00  "           Ploesti, Rumania
       "   29,   "     7:45  "           Wiener-Neustadt, Austria
       "   31,   "     8:45  "           Ploesti, Rumania
     June   2, 1944    7:00 Hrs.         Szoinok, Hungary
       "    5,   "     7:15  "           Fiornovo, Rumania
       "    6,   "     8:30  "           Ploesti, Rumania
       "   10,   "     6:00  "           Porta Marghira, Italy
       "   11,   "     8:15  "           Giurgiu, Rumania
       "   13,   "     7:15  "           Szona, Hungary
       "   23,   "     8:15  "           Giurgiu, Rumania
       "   25,   "     9:00  "           Avignon, France
       "   28,   "     8:30  "           Bucharest, Rumania
     July   5, 1944    Aborted           Beziers, France
       "    6,   "     6:15  "           Aviano, Italy
       "    8,   "     7:15  "           Vienna, Austria
       "   11,   "     7:30  "           Toulon, France
       "   12,   "     9:00  "           Nimes, France
       "   15,   "     8:30  "           Petfurdo, Hungary
       "   16,   "     7:30  "           Wiener-Nausdorf, Germany
     Total number of combat sorties........ 35
     Total number of combat flying hours..261:50


                                        William H. Tallant
                                        Capt. Air Corps
                                        Operations Officer
```

Dad's missions.

II

I remember a time when a girlfriend and I were giggling and laughing as we ran and ran up a grassy hill. Falling and rolling down the other side, we realized that the hairy monsters had stopped chasing us. We crept back up the hill and cautiously peeked over the top to see brown hairy monsters chained to stakes outside each little house. On our way from school, we had come upon some little houses and stopped to play in them. There were little beds, chairs and tables; we thought how lucky, some children were to have these playhouses. We pretended that they were ours. We sat in the chairs, had pretend tea at the tables, and even tried lying down on the little beds. We were ready to set up camp in our new-found playhouses. However, since we didn't know who they belonged to, we decided until we find out, we should leave. As we left, we saw a blur of brown-moving hair running toward us and that is when we started to run and ended up on the other side of the hill.

Apparently, while we were playing house, the occupants were out for a walk with their handlers. Upon return, they spotted us leaving and started a full run toward us. We didn't know what they were but sensing danger took off. Thank goodness we did, for these hairy monsters turned out to be primates, orangutans.

We stopped by these little houses every day after school. We played with our monsters from afar because they were chained to stakes. Sitting on the grass, we would throw balls, laugh, and watch them do all sorts of tricks. One day I put my schoolwork down a little too close to our new-found friends. One grabbed my books and started to shred my paperwork. I screamed, as I watched in horror.

At school the next day, the teacher could be heard by all saying, "What, a monkey ate your homework?" I was so embarrassed. However, I bet she never had that excuse before.

As I continued to enjoy the sun on my back, I started to reflect on my relationship with my husband. Spending time with my dad had stirred up some emotions that caused me to take a look at my discontent with him. I noticed how respectful my dad and uncle were to their wives. I think this brought my discontent in my marriage to the forefront.

I have always loved my life; the ups, downs, and the all arounds of it. I look at my life as a book, with many different chapters, and many different characters. Now, of course, I have enjoyed certain chapters more than others. However, I wouldn't rewrite any of the chapters in any way. My current chapter has been fun and exciting in ways I didn't know existed. However, there has always been something missing. I have felt something missing starting with the earliest chapters of my adult life.

This chapter started off really well. Meeting my husband in a Native American Indian store, I took as a sign that it was meant to be. I have been involved with the Native peoples for 30 years. Here was a man who collected and dealt in Native American Indian art. Wow, what a combination we would make. I knew the Native people's ways, and he knew their art. I soon learned that he was a producer of the largest Native American Indian Art and Antique show and sale in the country. I was impressed and relieved that he had a full life. It seemed that the men I had met over the years really didn't have their own passion, which made any relationship with them difficult. I have always had such a passion for

The children in my babysitting service.

Let that wind blow. Feels so good!

Captain's dinner

life and everything it offered. I am always looking for something new to discover. My life has always been very full, however, something always seemed to be missing.

When I was 14 years old, I started a morning babysitting service in our neighborhood. In the summer, when school was out, I wanted to do something. Too young to work, I learned the ways of an entrepreneur early. I canvassed the neighborhood to see if any mom was interested in having their children watched for four hours in the morning. The response was overwhelming. By the time I started, I had 10 children and it grew to 12. I elicited the help of a girlfriend, and we split the money every week. We would gather the children early and take them to the park and teach them games, do art projects, and just plain have fun. One day it started to rain, and we were running down the street to my house. We finished that morning in the basement of our house. My mom didn't want any of the children to wander around our house, so she told them she had a pet alligator that lived in the bathroom. From that day forward, none of those kids ever wanted to come into our house again. When they saw my mom in the neighborhood, they always asked how Charlie was, for that is the name my mom gave the alligator.

I got my zest for life from my mom. She was like that famous redheaded comedienne that was on television, and she had a best friend just like the one in the sitcom. Being out with them was interesting, to say the least. There were many funny times. I remember a time when mom and I went Christmas shopping.

Lady! Lady! Lady! What are you doing? I turned around and saw my mom lying across the threshold of the doorway, buried under a mound of Christmas packages. The glass door was opening and shutting, banging her on the head each time it opened and closed. The clerk was still yelling, but made no move to help her. It was snowing outside, we had been Christmas shopping for several hours, walking from store to store, battling the wind, and the snow, trying to find just the right presents for everyone in the family. On the way back to the car, I spotted just the right gift for someone on my list in a store window. Since we had so many packages, mom said she would stay outside with the packages. I found a ledge protected from the cold for her to sit on and then went into the store to get that perfect gift. The last place I saw my mom, she was sitting on the ledge outside the store with all of our packages around her. Now, she was lying on the floor with all the packages on top of her while a door was banging her on the head. As I helped her up, the owner never came over to see how she was.

He just said, "Lady, what are you doing?"

She replied, "What the heck do you think I'm doing, taking a nap?"

He didn't seem to hear her. He was only concerned about her causing trouble for him, rather than caring if she got hurt. As it turned out, mom was fine. We picked up all the packages, mom brushed herself off, and we left to battle the snow once again. I never did get that perfect gift.

Yesterday, I was on the island that was about parrots, pirates, and boats. Today was Honduras. Meeting new people and exploring new places. Our ship docked not far from the reef and we were transported by one of those boats that skim the water. The fauna are amazing and I especially enjoyed the dances performed by the Garifuna, a tribe of people who inhabit this part of the world. Punta, the style dance that they do, looked like fun and I had to hold myself from jumping in and joining them. Of course, I had to purchase some of their crafts, especially since it was jewelry. A girl just can't have enough, is my motto. Now back on the ship; time for dinner. I think I'll wear my new Garifuna handmade necklace.

I have been having some really disturbing thoughts on this trip. Disturbing, only because I really cannot act on the feelings I have. I have had a lot of alone time and realized that I really don't like my husband. I don't like him most of the time. He is sarcastic and disrespectful. He really has no interest in what I do or what I like. We don't have much, if anything, in common anymore. I'm not so sure we ever did. He had a lot of pain in his legs over the last couple of months, coupled with weakness in both causing him some problems with walking. Going from doctor to doctor, one specialist after another became so frustrating.

Finally, the doctors were able to diagnose the pain in his legs. My heart goes out to him, for to be told that you have a chronic nerve disease that is not reversible, is very difficult news to hear. At least the pain subsided before this trip, but I can tell walking is becoming more difficult for him. I have no idea what goes on in his mind or heart. When I left him a couple of years ago, he didn't seem to care. Yet, he wanted me to still be some sort of partner in his life. My mixed feelings have kept

Garifuna tribal dancers

Our ship is in the background.

Relaxing on the veranda.

A friendly pirate

me coming back each time I leave. That time I came back into his life because of his broken neck. He needed help and he had no one in his life that would assist him. Once again, he needs help, so here I am. I am on a lovely cruise, basically alone. However, there's the sun, the ocean and those wonderful massages to keep me company.

CHAPTER THREE

TOILET PAPER ART

GAIN I AM SITTING IN THE BACK OF A SQUAD CAR. Man, this was becoming a habit, a bad habit. This time I was concerned about what the next facility would be like. I was out of reception, and I was going to some sort of crisis type unit. Being arrested on Christmas Eve and missing Christmas day with Joyce and her family started to wear on me. She was going to pick me up. We were all going to have dinner together. I thought about the dinner they had and the presents under the tree that had been opened. I felt sad. There was always a gift for me. I fantasized about what that gift had been.

I thought about all the times that I had been part of their family celebrations. My most vivid memory was of Joyce's daughter's wedding. It was held in a yacht club on a lake. The sun's rays were shining on the water where ducks were taking their afternoon stroll. A boat appeared carrying her daughter and her bridesmaids. The sight was like something out of a movie. After the boat docked, each groomsman took the arm of a bridesmaid, helped them off the boat, onto the dock, and escorted them up to the deck of the yacht club. When Joyce's daughter left the boat, she was escorted by her dad. Once everyone was gathered on the patio deck, Joyce performed the ceremony. I was so excited to be part of this wonderful day. I had such a good time that day, of course I was drinking heavily and really got smashed. I danced every dance and felt so free! Free! I won't be experiencing that word for quite some time. I wondered if I would ever experience the joy of a wedding ceremony, a wife, and a marriage.

My memory was interrupted by something being held under my nose. It smelled awful and it really gave me a start. I had fainted and there was this cop hovering over me with a little bottle in his hand. I fainted again and that bottle was held under my nose once again. As I was being led into the prison, which looked like the buildings I've seen on television shows, someone said, "He is severely dehydrated." That is the last thing I heard before I passed out again.

I woke up with an IV in my arm and that helped me feel less faint. I came around and was escorted to a padded cell that had nothing in it. The toilet was a hole in the ground with some metal around it. I thought I had heard somewhere that the Arabs who live in the desert make a hole in the sand to relieve themselves. Where did that thought come from? I think Joyce might have told me that since she worked in Saudi Arabia at one time.

I was in an acute crisis unit of a prison to get some help. I didn't care. I was really angry. Angry because I had been railroaded in the first place and shouldn't be here. Hitting the wall felt good. I heard other inmates pounding as well. I guess we're all angry.

Toilet paper when rolled up works really well for art projects. Toilet paper doves, suns made out of carrots and even clouds appeared on one of my walls. On the other wall I made a heart with a tear drop inside with the words "feel my pain." My heart just ached, and creating was the only way I could express that pain.

The more I thought of that circus of a court room, the angrier I got. All the guards laughing at me just riled me up even more. To get back at all of them, after I ate my food and used my carrots for my suns, I crapped in one of the containers on my tray. "Boy, something smells bad on this tray", I heard the female guard say. They didn't find that funny, nor did it annoy them enough. So, I went back to pounding on the wall.

More words appeared on my wall. "Stop war and make peace" and "Can't escape the precious pain." I also wrote "The Lord knows my pain." I did this with red punch so it dripped down the wall like blood. However, my best piece of art was the outline of the continent of Africa. My anger was just a mask for my fear. I was so scared. I didn't know what was going to happen to me. The drugs kept me pretty drowsy. Paranoia started to take over. I found a home made rope in one of the cells I was moved to. Cells are supposed to be cleaned and cleared out after each inmate. Obviously this cell wasn't, or was it left there purposely. Did they want me to hang myself? Waving at the camera, I flushed it down the toilet.

Finally, I saw a doctor. That was the beginning of receiving some proper medication. It was determined that I was well enough to serve my time in a regular prison that had medical facilities rather than going to a prison hospital. After a five hour drive, I entered the facility where I spent the next four years.

That first year was really challenging for me, as I mentioned earlier. I acted out my anger in the most inappropriate ways. I was experimented on to determine the proper combination of medicines. I hung myself, but I don't want to discuss the details of that situation. It brings up too many horrific memories. Just suffice it to say, I was tended to and all ended well.

Experiencing abuse and racism caused me to start reflecting on my life. What the hell was I doing here? This is not where successful artists end up, except prison taggers. For the first time, I was serious about changing.

CHAPTER FOUR

BLONDE LADY FROM THE STATES

I LOVE THIS TIME OF YEAR IN SANTA FE. The weather is mild, the flowers are in bloom, and the distant mountains still have remnants of snow. So many galleries of art to explore, from antique to modern, done in every modality possible. Most of the high end galleries are on Canyon road, which is part of the old Santa Fe Trail, the famous trade route from the Midwest to the West. The road is partially paved. However, it still has that "old west" flavor. As I stroll down the road I imagine horses, mules, and wagons rolling alongside me. It's like I'm back in time.

Eating in this town is a palate's delight. My motto when I visit this town is "so many restaurants in so little time." Therefore, I overeat when I visit since I try to live up to that motto.

I am excited about seeing the new Native American and Ethnographic Antique Show and Sale. I love all the eclectic art, Mexican, Native American mixed in with Chinese, African, and Middle Eastern. Usually, I head for the Native American jewelry. However, walking around the show I spotted some art from the Middle East that looked interesting. As I approached the booth, my thoughts went to a time when I was in the Middle East. I started reminiscing about Saudi Arabia, Abu Dhabi, and Dubai.

Climbing down the stairs of the jet, my first sight was men standing all

Getting ready for camel racing.

around holding guns. I later found out the guns were M13s and that the Saudis considered airports military installations. It was a little put offing to be surrounded with so much artillery. My first introduction to this country was the heat, for when I walked through the door of the plane the heat hit me like I had just stepped into an oven.

It had to be over 100 degrees with humidity as high. All my senses were really getting a workout. There were horns honking, people all talking at the same time in many different languages, the smell of curry was everywhere along with smells that were not even familiar. It was challenging to walk as men were pulling on my suitcases asking if I needed someone to carry them. Heat, guns, sounds, smells made my head spin. What a culture shock!

A local hotel in Jeddah was my base. I learned very quickly that none of the males in our group could be in my room, or I in theirs, with the door closed. So, all of our business meetings were held with people walking by, even stopping to give us a warm greeting.

While shopping, I remember being pushed up against a wall as people were running in every direction and men were swinging sticks through the chaotic crowd while the sound of the minaret was blaring. Whew, I was safe from being trampled. When calling to worship sounds, the religious police, with their sticks make sure all stores are closed and owners as well as shoppers go to the mosque for prayer time. The clicking sound those sticks made as they hit the ground was like listening to crickets in the countryside. These religious police were herding the people just like if they were sheep. Although their herd was not cooperating for they were going in all different directions. My corporate guide had pushed me out of the way just in time before I was the recipient of a blow from one of those wielding clicking sticks.

We were on our way to the Saudi military base to interview some of the medical personnel we had hired, when we came upon an accident. Unlike here, everyone is in the wrong and all people involved, including passengers, are taken to their police station to sort things out. Everyone was talking at once and their voices were becoming louder and louder. You can just imagine all the chaos. It took a while, however, we were able to get passed the crumpled cars and angry people and continued on toward the base.

On our way, I realized I was bleeding, and I thought to myself, "I shouldn't have had that surgery last week". Here I was in a third world country, half way around the world, bleeding. Well, the good news was I was on my way to a hospital. What better place to have myself checked out. After all, I along with several other corporate staff members had hired only the best. So, I knew I would be in good hands, or least I hoped so.

Our Saudi driver pulled up to the guarded gate, rolled down his window, and spoke to the guards. With that, the gates opened and fingers pointed to where we were supposed to park our car. I felt the rush of cold air as I entered the hospital. It was like walking from an oven into a cooler, for it had to be 100 degrees outside and half that inside. My traveling partner and I were on our own. He sought out some doctors and I went toward the nurse's room.

As I was interviewing Karen, a physician's assistant, I interrupted the conversation and told her my dilemma. An American emergency doctor offered to check me out in Karen's office. An examining table with those all too familiar stirrups, a desk, a copying machine and a couple of chairs furnished her office.

There I was, feet in the stirrups, spread eagle, being examined, when all of a sudden the office door opened and a couple of workers came in to use the copy machine. When they left, the doctor apologized and said, "Welcome to our hospital." Karen told the workers to hurry up and leave. I figured while I had his attention, in a manner of speaking, I thought I might as well take the opportunity to interview him.

"So, Doctor Smith, how do you like your job here at this military hospital?"

He answered, never coming up from behind the sheet, "I love what I do." He continued with, "I wonder if that was an appropriate answer while I am examining you."

Our laughter was interrupted by two more workers coming to get something. The buzz around the hospital was "Go check out that blonde lady from the states" and many of them did. I got past my embarrassment, and chalked it up to just another adventure. Both the doctor and I had completed our job; he finished examining me and I had completed the interview process. As it turned out, my situation was not a serious one, just an annoying one. We both agreed that our encounter was an unusual one.

I thanked him and Karen, and I continued our business.

As I continued down the aisles of the show meandering through the many booths that were displaying and selling their antique art, I chuckled at that memory and wondered what ever happened to that doctor and Karen. So long ago!

CHAPTER FIVE

MY VERY OWN SKATES

I DECIDED THAT I WAS NOT GOING TO SIT AROUND waiting for my next peanut butter and jelly sandwich. I started attending as many programs as I could. I was learning how to manage my anger, started to realize what the drugs were doing to my brain and body, and became committed to staying out of trouble. During this time, I started thinking about my mom.

I was so close to my mom. I don't remember when I was born. However, I am sure from the moment she brought me home from Martin Luther King Hospital she and I were bonded in a very special way. Even though I was the second youngest of fourteen children, I always felt special. Our dad died when I was very small, and she was the one who held our family together. She had nicknames for us like Fella, Fellaman, Bow, Chuck Chuck, Bucky, Wee Wee, and mine, Chow. She looked at me with such love and when she held me I felt her warmth. I so longed for that kind of love and warmth again.

I remembered sleeping in my mom's room and that kept me close to her. I needed to feel my mom's security so I followed her all over. Wherever she went, there I was. She was my blanket. I knew I was mom's favorite and felt especially loved by her. When she got sick, I went as often as I could to the hospital for her treatments. However, during that time feelings of sadness crept in. I was scared that my security was threatened. Not having a dad magnified those feelings. Even though I had many siblings to play with, it got lonely at times, since we younger boys were not allowed to play outside. She protected us from the gang and rough elements of the projects in Los Angeles.

I learned later that my mom had a reputation in the Jordan Downs Projects as a tough lady, no one to mess with. I'm not sure if this was true, but somewhere I heard that Mom used to make the neighborhood gang members pull their pants down just to mess with them. She would hold a shotgun on them while they did what she asked. They used to call her "Mama". She was notorious and known as the "mama" of the projects.

I remembered a time I went shopping with mom and saw a toy robot that I really wanted. As I got older, I realized she probably did not have the money, and did without something, just to get me the robot. I really loved that robot. It was blue, black, and red. It walked and shot its gun.

My nurturing now came from the letters that I received from the lady that I came to love and looked at as a mom figure. Those letters kept me going. I learned later, that she loved receiving good news from me, and saved all the certificates and drawings that I sent to her. I kept thinking she had to care about me, and wanted only the best for me. I needed to believe that. After all, she hung in there with me over a 10 year period, at which time I was drugging and drinking. I met her in a locked medical facility, when she came to visit someone else. I came to rely on that love for security. I needed it!

I thought about the times I visited her and her husband for dinners or swimming. I sure appreciated the money that her husband sent me, and I looked forward to the packages that came from Joyce. They usually were chalk full of goodies, my favorite being those rolls with icing and cinnamon on them.

My interest in art started out with the typical coloring book and crayons. However, my interest became stronger and stronger as I was able to express myself through creativity. Art became my outlet when I was young. It became my outlet once again as I created cards and drew on the letters that I sent to Joyce. Expressing myself in that way was much healthier than my previous artwork. Well, toilet paper art really isn't my thing anyway!

As time went on and more packages came, I just knew that Joyce and her husband loved me. They would not have done those things if they didn't. I was starting to feel secure just knowing that. I reviewed my relationship with both him and her and recognized, and maybe for the first time really understood the level of her commitment. She had visited me regularly in each board and care facility and in jail. A couple of times she went to court for me and even tried to work with my public defender. She stayed in contact with me the entire four and a half years, while I was in prison. Even though I did not have my family in my life, I was blessed and appreciated having someone in my life who cared so deeply.

The next three years I went to as many classes as I could. Between the classes, my exercise program, and the letters from Joyce, life became easier for me. I no longer thought of acting out, for I came to learn how to channel my energy in positive ways. There were still incidents that caused me concern. However, being anti-social really served me well.

I met people in prison who knew my mom and brothers. I learned that my brother, Ray, who I had not seen for ten years, had been in prison and may be on the street. Sadness, once again crept over me. I missed him so much. I missed both of my brothers, Ray and Chris, that I grew up with in all the group homes. I thought back to the times when I was with my family, and even though times were tough, we were together.

Memories of my family came flooding back. I reflected on the time mom decided to move us out of the projects, and into a house. However, her illness was becoming more and more serious and threatening. Lack of money became an issue and since paying the rent became impossible, eviction was the only option for us

A hotel was our home for the next several months. However, we moved so often it was hard to keep track of where we were to sleep at night. In one place we had just one bed, which we gave to our mom. We were all used to sleeping four in a bed; however, after we gave the bed to mom, the floor is where we all slept. The good thing about the floor was there was more room to stretch out.

Our moves included friends' homes and motels until social workers took my older brother, Chris, and me away from our family. I was around seven years old. My younger brother, Ray, had already gone to live with one of our older sisters, her boyfriend, and her two children.

The only story I remember my mom telling me was that one of her friends jumped out a window. There were times I would think to myself, a normal family does not talk or act the way my family talked and acted. Although, looking back at that, I don't know how I knew what a normal family would act like. However, beating a child because they had an accident, letting a small child watch movies that were much too violent for them to watch, or just the over the top discipline that occurred to my brothers, just didn't seem normal.

Our food, most of the time, was limited to rice and beans, which mom bought with the monies she got from the church. Social workers were always checking us out. Although, we didn't mind the social workers coming at Christmas with presents. This guy would come with a tree and a whole lot of presents for all of us. We would play with our new stuff and have lots of fun. Being so young, I don't remember, however, I'm sure that he brought all the food for our Christmas dinner as well. Christmas time was a happy time for us. I remember one year we all got skates. That was a big deal to me, my very own skates.

I sure was learning a lot about myself just by being locked up, however, I really started to get the picture while attending the groups. I was an alcoholic and had to accept the fact that I could not control my drinking. I got it! I knew when I got out I needed to keep working on myself in that area. Deep inside me there was a loving and kind person that I needed to continue to nurture. I liked that person and I didn't like the person who showed up when I was drinking and drunk.

I kept pretty much to myself for protection from conflicts of any kind. I did push ups every day to keep my mind from going to a place that would cause me to become depressed. Physical exercise helped me emotionally as well as mentally.

Even though I kept to myself, when I got my packages, I would share some of my food with others. Joyce sent me a Christmas package that had all kinds of fun stuff in it. I especially liked the Christmas candies. In fact, I saved them. I tried not to think about how I screwed up, got arrested on Christmas Eve, and missed out on my Christmas outing with Joyce. I just kept thinking about the day I would get out and celebrate Christmas with Joyce and her family. They always had good food and nice presents for me.

I pictured myself sitting at the dining table eating turkey, and sitting by their tree opening all my gifts. That picture kept me going.

CHAPTER SIX

GOATS, GAMES AND ROOSTERS

G ET OUT OF MY CAR!" "Stop!" "Come on, stop tearing that paper!" Getting that goat out of my car was quite a challenge. I have had goats climb up on top of my car or walk across my car, but this was a first. It was my fault; I had left the tailgate door open when I got this family's Christmas gifts. I knew better, but I was in a hurry to bring in gifts to this family.

Even though I had been coming to the Navajo reservation for many years during the holiday season, it always felt like the first time. I loved being one of Santa's helpers and seeing the joy in the faces of children when Santa handed them their gifts. The twinkle in the eyes of the elders who danced with glee when getting their new sweater or shawl always brought a tear to my eye.

As I proceeded to get the rest of the gifts out of the van, I started to reminisce about the time that changed my life forever. It started with a visit to a small boarding school in a remote area of the reservation. I, along with a few of my friends, had brought in what we called, "Santa bags." Each bag was filled with toys and clothing for a few families that needed a little extra help.

One person always played Santa and the rest of us were his helpers. Santa and helpers personally delivered these bags along with turkeys and all the trimmings for a holiday dinner. We stayed with a Navajo lady who would translate for us when necessary, as well as help us navigate the rough terrain. Since that visit, I have continued to visit this little community during the holiday season with friends who want to experience the joy of giving.

We had just finished our "Santa visits" and were on our way back to Hazel's house, when Hazel asked us if we could stop to see a family she had recently discovered was in trouble. So, even though, we had no more gifts, since "Santa" still had his suit on, we decided to stop and have Santa play with whatever children we found there.

Trailing two sets of tire tracks leading to a small house nestled up to a hill, our vehicle propelled its way through the muddy mixture of snow and gravel that once had been some sort of road. Cold, hungry, dogs greeted us with wagging tails that hung between their legs, and hearts that were obviously broken by one too many defeats. Watching the dogs and chickens fight over the last of our five pound bag of dog food, wondering how they survive in this desolate place, we entered this broken down house through the back door. Standing in the kitchen, next to the only piece of furniture, a table filled with chopped wood, was a little girl with eyes filled with wonder and a smile that was infectious. A boy, about twelve years old, wearing a shirt that was too small, stood in front of the living room window that was covered with plastic. He was smiling and seemed to be feeling a sense of excitement brought on by our appearance. A boy, who looked like he was a couple of years younger, stood very close to him, feeling some apprehension, with another little one in diapers, who seemed perplexed by the goings on.

My heart became heavy and filled with pain as I spotted an albino boy around seven, only wearing a shirt and a pair of shorts, no socks, or shoes. He was standing alone trying to look up, but due to the light that was coming in through the window, was unable to do so. I knew immediately that he was an old soul, someone who was sent here to teach the world compassion and our oneness with each other.

A woman sat on the edge of one of the three beds, looking down at the dingy wood floors. She looked like she was feeling very confused and a bit embarrassed by our presence. However, the appearance of Santa Claus brought looks of disbelief, wariness, and joy to all of their faces.

34

Santa took his rightful place in a big overstuffed chair and motioned to the little girl with the infectious smile to join him. With exaltation she climbed up on his knee and nestled herself in his lap. I could tell she was feeling like a queen and her smile just got bigger when she saw the picture of herself with Santa Claus.

As I took each child's picture, I could feel my adrenaline flowing and became high from the love that was emitting from all the hearts in the room. Even though this little shabby house was dim and obscure, there seemed to be a light that was not coming from outside through the windows, but from inside, through all of us.

When Santa emptied his bag of the few remaining golden books and stuffed animals, an overwhelming sense of sadness fell upon me as I realized Santa did not have what this family really needed. Leaving with heavy hearts and tears streaming down the face of one of Santa's helpers, we waved goodbye to the little faces that were pushed up against the one and only windowpane. We knew what we had to do.

Walking the aisles of the little trading post with $102.50, all the money that we had collectively, the Christmas turkey dinner, with all the trimmings, started to appear in our cart, along with little cars, puzzles, games, coloring books and crayons. Peanut butter and jelly even found their way into the carrier. As we headed back, the words "over the snow and through the woods to grandma's house we go…" kept going through my mind, connecting me with the warm feelings from the past.

Prevailing over the muddy ruts that led to the sounds of drumming and singing, we stopped in front of what looked like a Hogan. That was my first of many experiences with a sweat lodge. Hazel climbed out of our vehicle and headed towards the small draped opening of the round canvassed hut like building. A head popped through the draped opening, looking very confused and as she listened to Hazel, exited the little hut. As she approached our vehicle, I was feeling just as confused as she looked, for I had no idea why we had stopped here. It became clear to me as it was explained that this lady was the grandmother, and head of the family, that we were going back to Grandma Clay. She had been part of a prayer ceremony held by the community's medicine man since early that morning.

The little faces that had been at the window were now hanging out the door, with eyes and smiles that lit up with wonder and hope, as they watched us stop and unload the brown paper bags. Emotions were high as these barefooted little angels looked at all the food and toys.

Puzzles made their way to the floor, toy cars began being pushed, and the peanut butter was immediately tasted. Chills covered my entire body and my eyes filled with tears as we learned that Grandma Clay had not just been a part of the prayer ceremony, she was the reason that there was a prayer ceremony.

The medicine man, his singer, drummers, and several people from the community, had been praying since dawn to the Great Spirit for food for her family. Disbelief and gratitude covered her face as she looked around the room at the children playing with their newfound treasures, and at the turkey and the canned goods that were sitting on the table, and at us. She was in awe of how fast the Great Spirit answered her prayers, and looked upon us as a gift from God. Whether we were manifestations of her prayers and God's gift to her, or just Anglos that happened to find their way onto the reservation, it didn't really matter. What did matter was the love that was exchanged between us, and how this experience changed all of our lives.

There was one incident that did not bring the kind of joy that I was used to experiencing on my visits. As I climbed up the cinder blocks which were makeshift stairs that preceded the wooden door, I noticed a beautiful rooster. That sight took me back a bit, since I had never seen a rooster on the reservation. The colors on him were vibrant blues, reds, and greens. We all commented on him and entered the door into a room that had lots of small children jumping up and down at the sight of Santa. As Santa passed out gifts from his bag, I noticed some of the toys needed batteries. I had a stash of them in my van, so I left to go retrieve them. As I walked toward my car, I noticed the rooster out of the side of my eye, charging me, but it was too late to dodge him. I felt his beak enter my skin right by my knee and my legs gave way. I managed to get myself to the car before he got me again. I was pissed and started throwing anything that I could grab at him to keep him at bay. My only weapons were empty water bottles. As I was attempting to protect myself, my friend came to my rescue. She grabbed some of the presents and started swinging games, balls, whatever we had, at him. He finally gave up and left us alone. Blood trickling down my leg, hobbling, I continued on as one of Santa's helpers. After all, can't keep a good elf down.

Reservation road

One of our Santa stops

Home of the rooster

So happy with new clothes.

Playing with their new toys.

Goats, goats and more goats.

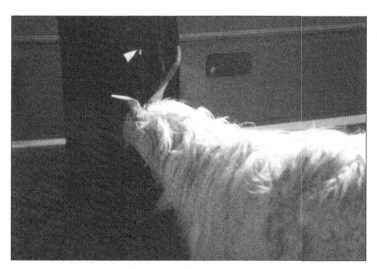

Checking out Santa's goodies.

One tired Santa.

CHAPTER SEVEN

IT ALL BEGAN WITH A TEDDY BEAR

I WAS SCARED AND DID NOT KNOW WHAT TO MAKE of all what was going on. A nurse checked me for lice, took care of my ringworm by washing my hair with some special soap, checked my body, and weighed me. I was not only scared, but also humiliated. The uniform that the staff gave me to wear consisted of blue jeans and a gray shirt with a picture of arms wrapped around a teddy bear. A sheet and a blanket were given to me, and then I was shown to my bed. Life did not seem real. Fear, confusion, and sadness caused many a sleepless night. There was harsh discipline, bordering on abuse and neglect. I felt abandoned and alone.

What a traumatic experience that was for my brother and me. We were told we were going out for hamburgers, which never happened. Instead, we ended up in a child protection institution, a place for abused, neglected, or abandoned children. Otherwise, an orphanage and a couple steps above the orphanage asylums of the earlier centuries. The institution had come to replace a former polio hospital in a time when polio was becoming less of a health threat and over time updated to accommodate more children. Floodlights, a 14-foot chain link fence, topped with five feet of wire mesh (barbed wire) surrounded the grounds. This was my new home and in some ways, my new family, only instead of 13 brothers and sisters, I now had hundreds.

Here I am, once again, in a facility with bars, barbed wire, and another new family, while still feeling alone and abandoned. The only difference between the uniforms is the teddy bear is missing on my current one. Again, feelings of fear, confusion, and sadness are causing many a sleepless night.

I came to realize during my time at the orphanage that even though my mom did her best, there were times when enough food for all of us was not always possible. We all would drink a lot of water to fill us up so the food would last. I saw things that a small child should not see. I was aware of some situations that were not proper for a small child. I thought about my two sisters I never really got to know. Because of their retardation, they went to live in a special home.

After a couple of months, my older brother and I went to a foster home. Actually, a self-help group home in Compton. A husband and wife ran the home that housed eight children from ages eight to eighteen years of age. My younger brother, who was with my older sister, eventually joined us. We were there for the next five years.

Over those next five years, I experienced a myriad of emotions. Sadness when I started to think and realize what had happened to me. I missed my family. Mom died during the first year I was at the group home. Dressed in an outdated outfit that included bell-bottom pants, the staff took me to her funeral. My sisters made fun of how I was dressed. I did not care, because I was dressed in clothes that were from mom's era, and that, for me, overshadowed the negative comments. That might have been the beginning of my ability to take the focus off the negative and try to find a positive in a negative comment or situation. That survival technique served me well, especially where I find myself now.

Even though I was going to as many classes as I could in prison, and getting a lot out of them, school was very difficult for me. I did not start school until somewhere around third grade. By the time I was in eighth grade, the work became extremely difficult and I could not to continue. Actually, I ditched school most days. When I did graduate elementary school, my desire was to become a successful artist. As I got older, the gang life became more exciting to me.

One day I came home, and just as I was just about to go through the front door was told that there were repairs going on. I would need to go around to the back door. When I opened the door, I heard "surprise" and felt the party atmosphere. It was for me! That party when I turned 10 brought me a real sense of happiness. Birthday parties were special. They still are, unfortunately, I haven't had one for a long time.

Another happy time came when I received an electronic toy that I had really wanted. I started to feel cared for and loved. Making tents in my room, coloring, and playing games made for more happy memories. I learned how to charm my way around a situation, and I used that charm to get what I wanted. That did serve me pretty well, especially with the woman who ran the group home. We went to plays and sporting events. Then there was the yearly motor home trip to the desert, which included a hotel visit. We all looked forward to that yearly trip. Camp was also a yearly event, one that I really looked forward to and had great fun. The first night we slept in cabins. When we would take hikes we would sleep outdoors. Although there were these happy times, nothing or no one could replace my mom or my family. In a way, I fantasized about this being my family, as I am sure we all did, even though we all were very aware of the reality that we found ourselves.

Sadness and happiness were interrupted by intermittent feelings of fear. Fear of the unknown. Fear of the neighborhood, in which I found myself. Fear of what was going to happen to me and to my brothers. My younger brother was intrigued with the gang life and really developed his fighting skills. When I didn't find my brother home after school, I worried about him getting beat up or killed until he walked through the door. I was in constant fear over this. He was my lifeline, even though, some of the time we went our separate ways. Growing up in the neighborhoods I found myself in was very dangerous. Drive by shootings were common and I always had to be aware of my surroundings.

Kicking it outside was not relaxing. I hated the sound of the helicopters that would fly over the neighborhood and the intermittent gunfire always gave me chills. I knew something was coming down and just hoped it wouldn't involve my surroundings. Gosh, I missed…not sure what I missed. I guess I just wanted to feel safe and yet, I couldn't remember when I ever did. My mom used to make me feel safe, and yet, I know that was a young boy's fantasy.

As time went on, I was getting into many fights, drinking and smoking weed. I hung out with gang members, ditched school, and found that life fun and exciting.

All through elementary school, I thought I would be something important in life, like a successful artist. I once drew a picture for a school contest and won first place. For the same contest, I drew a picture for a friend and he won second place. However, when I entered junior high school it was a completely different ball game. I was hanging out with gang members and I wanted to be like them. These guys were from a different gang from my background so I really couldn't join the gang, but they let me hang out with them anyway. I found that life exciting.

I have a much different perspective on that life from where I am now, in prison.

#
RICE, A PINK CHICKEN, AND A BOWL OF WARM MILK

WHEN I HEARD WE WERE GOING TO BE LEAVING Georgia to go to California, I had a flurry of emotions. Part of me was feeling sad, for I knew that would mean leaving Linda, my best friend and her family.

Linda was one of seven children. I don't remember where she was in relationship to the oldest or youngest; however, I do believe she was either the oldest or close to it. She and her six brothers and sisters slept in two beds, a double, and a twin. They all had to go to bed at the same time, which was very early. I never understood why, until one night I peeked in their bedroom window. I saw all the kids, including Linda, in their nightclothes. They each took their places in the two beds, some with their heads at the top, and some with their heads at the bottom. Whichever the case, they seemed to have it all worked out.

Dinners at Linda's house usually consisted of rice. Her mom would heap rice into a mound onto my plate, then place butter at the top of the mound, which would melt down the sides and all through the rice. Linda's

Our 1942 Dodge and the row house Georgia community we lived in.

Our new home in Pismo Beach, California.

family was poor, yet there was always enough food to include me in their mealtimes, or enough candy to add to my Easter basket or Christmas stocking. I remember one Easter, Linda and her family brought over an Easter Basket and a little pink baby chicken for me. The father had gotten each one of his children a baby chicken and included me as well. That always touched me, for I knew that they really didn't have the money to be buying me anything. I loved and nurtured that chicken and then one day it became ill and started to shake. My mom tried everything to make it well, from feeding it medicine from an eyedropper to heating it up in a pan. Nothing worked, and my little chicken died. Later we found out it was because of the dye that had been used to color the chicken.

As we packed up our 1942 Dodge, I started to become excited about our new adventure. Everything was in, the dog and I took our perspective places in the back seat, and we were off. As we became closer to where we were ultimately going to live, we all became very anxious to find our new home. It had been a long drive from Georgia to California coupled with the fact that our dog became ill with the chills just before Las Vegas.

Our dog was a medium sized German Shepard mixed with dingo and could be feisty. All though the desert the dog kept shaking and getting shocked every time he touched his nose to the metal strip around the car window. By the time we pulled into Las Vegas we all were feeling the heat of the desert, hungry and tired. My mom went and got Rex some warm milk from a restaurant and after a while he seemed to get better. I don't remember what all actually happened, but I do know that my parents were worried that Rex had distemper. Whether or not he did have distemper, I don't know, however, that dog lived another ten years. My mom never forgot the love and concerns the restaurant owner had for our dog, who actually gave my mom the milk and told her she could have whatever else she wanted. Rex obviously got well. Who knows if it was the warm milk or the love and concern that were bestowed on him?

The ocean was so big and beautiful, and the sight of the mountains was breathtaking. I remember pulling into a town that had lots of trees and hills. After several stops at different real estate offices, we drove out of that town, along a highway that rimmed the ocean into Pismo Beach. Pismo Beach is where we spent the rest of our time while my dad was in the army.

#101- PISMO BEACH, CALIF

#119- POMEROY ST. PISMO BEACH, CALIF

52# SUN BATHERS ON THE CLEAN WIDE BEACH
PISMO BEACH, CALIF

Pismo Beach, California in 1951

48

We met up with several other families that had been with us in Georgia, at what looked like a motel. It was a motel. There were enough of us to rent out all of the rooms. That was home. It was furnished, and all of our personal belonging were on a moving truck somewhere along Route 66. I remember waiting for my games and all my stuff for what seemed like weeks, which really turned out to be just a couple of days.

The first couple of nights I was terrified of the noise that the ocean made hitting the retaining wall several blocks away. It sounded like the ocean waves were hitting our building. To put my mind at ease, my mom took me into town one day so I could see how far away the wall was from us. What an ominous sight. It was scary to me to think that wall was the only thing separating us from the huge waves that came in at night. I realized later that the wall was there to protect the city from the erosion that occurs from the high tides that come in at night.

The pier had a swing that hung in such a way that when I would swing on it, I could catch some of the waves. I loved it. I spent a lot of time down on the beach by the pier. The air was so warm that I could go into the water with my dress on, splash around chasing waves, come out and by the time I walked home, my clothes would almost be dry. This land was certainly different from any I had ever been to. Waves to chase, warm weather, mountains, and flowering shrubs all around.

I really didn't have any friends at Pismo Beach. I spent a lot of my time with an elderly blind man who lived around the corner from us. I would sit on his porch steps with him and he would tell me stories. All of his stories seem to have some sort of moral to them. I don't remember any of them in detail, but I do remember one. Actually, it wasn't a story, but an answer to a question that I had asked. Being ten years old and very curious, I asked him if he had always been blind.

He told me that he had sight once and that he had taken his sight for granted. "When you look at a tree," he said, "look at every part of that tree with not only your physical eyes, but with the eyes of your heart, as well." Being 10 years old, I really didn't understand what he was telling me. He went on to say, "Look at the bark of the tree, look closely and see all the life forms that move up and down the bark, and feel your oneness with them. When you look at the limbs of the tree, feel them; see them as part of the world around you. Look closely at the leaves and see the veins in each leaf. You see, when I had my sight, I looked at the tree, but never really saw it. Now that I can't see, I can only see the trees in my heart. Don't take your sight for granted. When you look at something around you in nature, really take the time to see it and feel it, for when you feel it; you are seeing it with the eyes of your heart. You and I are part of the beauty around us—don't take it for granted." I have never forgotten those words and have tried to live my life as he suggested.

That year, I suspect, was the beginning of my spiritual journey. A journey that began with the love that came from a poor family in Georgia, the love my mom showed me by trying so hard to help my chicken, the love that the restaurant owner showed our dog and the stories that an elderly blind man shared with a lonely 10-year-old girl.

Rice, a pink chicken, a warm bowl of milk and an elderly blind man taught me the meaning of unselfish love.

CHAPTER NINE

PING PONG BALL

MY BEST FRIEND IN GRADE SCHOOL, who I had lost touch with due to all my moves, was here.

I couldn't believe it. He was my very best friend. We ran the streets together. He was serving two life sentences. When he told me that, I got chills. Gosh, what if we had stayed in touch, what if we had still been running around. That could be me. I learned that a rival gang member had killed his brother and he took revenge. That revenge cost him his freedom.

Thinking back to our time together brought to mind another person who I thought was my friend. I guess he was jealous of our friendship because he caused trouble for me by lying to my friend about an incident that never took place. That lie caused me to be jumped and beaten up. My friend must have had some doubt, otherwise, I would have been killed. Seeing my friend brought back so many memories from that time of my life. What was I doing here?

Upon graduation from eighth grade, to keep me on the right path, the woman at the group home sent me to a Christian school. Practicing the teachings was difficult for me. I was busy smoking weed and drinking. My mind was blocked. Even though it was hard to understand what they were teaching me at that time, I knew there was a God and I knew who God was. I got frustrated and cursed at a teacher, and they suspended me from school. That was the end of that group home and the continuation of a self-destructive path.

They tried to keep us together. We were constantly shuffled between

My brothers and me

the orphanages and group homes. Sometimes two of us would be in the same place, but leaving one brother out. I felt like a ping pong ball. Back and forth…here and there…back and forth. My older brother, Chris, and I went to a treatment center that eventually took in all three of us. Ray, Chris, and I were there for the next four years. This is the longest we were together, and in one place. We thought we would be there, together, forever. My brothers were my lifeline. We became so close during this time. It was heartbreaking when this group home closed. It was the last time we were all together in one place.

When I was there, I thought it was cool that the staff let us smoke weed and do things that most parents would not. Looking back at those supposed good times I realize that those times set some beliefs about what was right and wrong. Unfortunately, I learned the hard way that drinking, smoking weed, and just hanging out doesn't really lead anywhere good. Video games are fun, but in most cases that doesn't lead to a fulfilling life, as I have ultimately learned.

When that group home closed, I landed back at the orphanage. My older brother, Chris, went to live with one of our sisters. After my short stint at the orphanage, I ended up in another group home for eight months, then back to the orphanage. Again, like a ping pong ball pinging back and forth. Although I did love being in that last group home because I loved all the attention I got from the girls in the town where the group home was. I had so many girlfriends, which was important to me at that time. My younger brother got his GED, graduated, moved to Palm Desert, started working, and had a girlfriend. I still was plodding along in my life.

I stayed at the orphanage for a few more months, continued with my bad behavior, and found myself in and out of psych hospitals due to depression. I do have some good memories from there. One memory is of a girl who I had a crush on. She was 17 and I was 16. She was blonde, had blue eyes, a great figure, and wore tight jeans that really showed it, and a nice personality. Recreation nights were always fun. We got to watch videos, play basketball, had coloring contests, and got to drink sodas, and eat candy. I loved the dances we had. The girl that I had a crush on was the most beautiful girl there and was always with me which made all the other guys jealous. I liked that. It made me feel important. When the orphanage finally closed, after many years of investigation, I ended up on the street. It all began with that teddy bear.

CHAPTER TEN

HOUSE OF GOYA

P ACKING UP MY MOM'S DOLLS FOR SHIPPING brought back so many memories. Mom made me promise that I would take care of her dolls, since she couldn't take them to the nursing home. So, they are going to be joining my dolls in California. Mom got me involved with collecting dolls right after my daughter was born. She eased me into it by suggesting I buy collector's dolls for my daughter, which I did. Then it progressed to antique dolls for me. That is how my addiction began.

I remember bringing my year old daughter to meet my mom at this little doll shop once a week for doughnuts and coffee, where the owner would show us a couple of new antique dolls that she had just acquired. Mom would pick one and put it away on lay-a-way until she could pay it off. We did this for weeks and weeks, until one day I decided I would buy my first antique doll. I paid $85 for that doll and thought that I was crazy. It took me several months to pay that doll off and she finally came home with me. The first thing I did was get her cleaned up and got her some new clothes. Look at me. I am playing with dolls, when I have a real life doll to play with. I was crazy, and got crazier with this new interest.

I started going to doll shows, buying dolls that I could not afford and then tried to figure out how to pay for them. Blue eyes, brown eyes, brunettes, and blondes found their way into my heart, then into my home. Oh, how I loved them.

My best friend came from this interest. My mom went to a little doll shop and told the lady that she and I would be great friends, and yes, I met her and we spent the next 37 years playing, talking, traveling and even working together. We started going to thrift stores looking for old dolls to clean up to sell in her shop.

Here I was a new doll collector. As all good doll collectors do, I went out junking looking for old dolls. My first experience junking for dolls was an experience that could have been my last. A friend and I, along with my two year old daughter, drove up and parked in front of a dilapidated building which had a little antique shop in the front. The neighborhood looked like the back lot of a movie studio with buildings that looked like facades and all sorts of colorful characters walking around. As we approached the shop, it became very evident that it was more of a junk shop, rather than an antique store. Our attempt to see what was beyond the dirty windows and broken door was to no avail. The shop was closed.

"Will be open soon" were the words scribbled on the note taped to the door. We decided to wait. We saw a little coffee shop on the corner, looked at each other questioningly and started down the street to try a cup of their brew.

After positioning ourselves on the bar stools, trying to avoid puddles of "whatever" on the floor, we ordered two cups of coffee and a coke for my daughter. We queried the clerk about the little antique store, however, got no helpful information as to when the store would be open. After paying the check, we walked back to the little shop.

As we approached the entrance a small, strange looking woman met us. She had red hair that grew in sparse little patches on her head. She greeted us with "Who are you and what do you want?" I noticed she had only one tooth. This was on the top, centered like it had just been placed there. What was so interesting about that tooth was that it was filed to a point. I thought, "Why would anyone file their one and only tooth to a point?" It was then I realized how Hansel and Gretel must have felt when they met the witch at the candy house.

We told her we would like to see her old dolls and assured her we were there to buy. With that, she unlocked the padlock, opened the door, and told us to go in. An old mangy bulldog hobbled over to us. "Meet Goya," the little woman said. My daughter, excited to see the dog, ran over and put her arms around him. He liked her, and started licking her face immediately. Goya looked like he hadn't eaten for a month, and I was hoping he wouldn't decide that my daughter would make a tasty lunch. The lady assured me that Goya would not hurt my child, as he had no teeth. My only concern then was how would I ever get her clean.

I picked up my daughter and put her in a chair in the middle of the room, instructed her not to get off and left her playing with Goya. My friend and I decided to plow through the piles of dolls as quickly as possible, and since the dolls were so dirty, it didn't take us long to start looking like them.

While I was trying to think of another way to go through the dolls without touching them, I heard a voice say, "Do you have any warlock rings?" I looked up and saw a man in his late 20s, about 6', with wild, unruly hair, wearing jeans and a shirt that needed washing badly. He repeated his original question to the lady who seemed very apprehensive.

I could tell she did not trust him. While asking him what a warlock ring was, she started to put all the loose jewelry away. By the way she was behaving it was apparent that she felt that she was going to be robbed. Funny thing, I had the same feeling.

While I was visualizing being held at gunpoint and wondering how I was going to handle this situation, my friend started questioning the man, as to what a warlock ring was. He told her he was a warlock and needed a warlock ring. I thought he meant he belonged to some sort of gang by the name of the Warlocks. However, this is not what he meant. He started to inform my friend and the lady, who by now had every loose piece of jewelry locked up, that he was a male witch. Well, I wanted to laugh, but had the good sense not to. With his last comment my friend started to challenge him and said, "Well, if you are a warlock then do something— like magic or something." I wanted to stuff something in her mouth.

I couldn't believe she was not only carrying on a conversation with this guy, but now she was antagonizing him. While the young man was going on and on about what a warlock is, the lady started yelling, "Get out, get out!" My daughter and Goya were still playing and sharing a package of small candies, I just stood there watching, and listening when all of a sudden, a man, who obviously had way too much to drink, staggered into the doorway and fell face down flat on the floor.

The lady started kicking at the man telling him to get up and out of the doorway. While she was kicking him, another man walked up and started to pull the man out of the store. I heard his head hit the metal piece that separated the inside of the store from the sidewalk. While the stranger continued to pull the poor man by his feet onto the sidewalk, the young man claiming to be a warlock started yelling "Get me out of here, get me out here. This place is jinxed" and jumped over the man who was being pulled out of the store and ran away.

I couldn't believe all what had just taken place and was trying to sort it all out in my mind when something caught my eye. I turned toward the pile of dolls and saw something fall from the ceiling. When it hit the floor, it kept going. I slowly looked up toward the ceiling and saw several more of these things. They were cockroaches. They were everywhere. Crawling, falling, scurrying all while I just stood there in shock.

At this point, I asked the lady what she wanted for all of her dolls, she told me, it seemed fair, so I paid her, picked up my daughter, packed the car and left the House of Goya.

CHAPTER ELEVEN

FOURTEEN DOLLARS

FTER SLITTING MY WRISTS, I found myself in a psych hospital. From then on, I went from one psych hospital to another until I finally ended up in a locked private facility where I met a beautiful Navajo girl. My life was about to change. Change in ways that I couldn't have dreamed possible.

She had the most beautiful long dark brown hair, almost black. Her eyes were so big and beautiful; I sensed a familiarity in them. She had a similar illness. Hers was coupled with promiscuity, due to being molested throughout her young life. This caused her to go from room to room and have sex with the different patients. I thought when she and I started hanging out together and became boyfriend and girlfriend, she would stop that behavior. I thought by us being a couple she would stop her bed hopping. I was wrong. Even though we were together, she would go into the different wards and visit other men. That just broke my heart. She would come back remorseful and would cry and promise not to do that anymore. This really messed with my mind. I knew that this was not normal behavior for being in a loving relationship; however, I always excused her behavior away. In the meantime, my heart was really hurting, and my mind was getting more and more messed up. She would promise me that she would stop having sex with other men. That promise could never be kept, because her illness always took over. This dysfunctional relationship lasted a couple of years.

When Joyce came to visit her Navajo daughter, I was excited to meet her. The first thing she said to me was "My, you are very handsome." Those words have stuck with me since then.

My Navajo girlfriend and I left the facility together and went to a board and care as a couple. We had a real nice room that I decorated. I used my creative side while there. I drew pictures for our wall, and for the wall of the administrative office. She and I had a good thing going. Joyce would come down on the weekends to take us out to lunch and sometimes we would go back to her house and spend the weekend. Dinners, swimming, movies were always options for us. Sometimes, it was hard to go back to the board and care.

We started to panhandle to buy alcohol and drugs. We both started drinking; I started to drink more heavily and ended up threatening a resident for fourteen dollars. It wasn't even worth it. The manager called the police and turned me in. This just propelled me further along the path of self-destruction. There I was, in my boxers, handcuffed, heading toward the back seat of a squad car. How embarrassing and humiliating. Arrested, charged with a felony robbery, I served four months and 20 days of a year's sentence.

When I was released, they just put me out on the street, no money, but more importantly, no medication. There I was, standing in front of the jail, alone, not knowing what to do or where to go. Then I realized I had Joyce's telephone number. She came down to see me several times while I was in jail. I came to look forward to those visits. I found someone who had a phone and I called Joyce. She had just gotten married that day; however, both she and her husband came down to get me. They had been together on and off for many years. I was grateful to have both of them in my life. Yet that did not stop me from picking up where I left off, drinking and using drugs, even though I hated my stay in jail.

A board and care in Compton was my next stop. I remember the first night I arrived. The room I was to sleep in was small, had a bed, dresser and a lamp. As I climbed into bed the smell of pee was overwhelming. It was obvious the sheets had not been changed on the bed; however, I was so tired that I just crashed. My girlfriend joined me after a month or so and we continued our drinking and using. We got involved with drug dealers and I stole electronics to feed my addictions. Too much crack/

cocaine got us shipped off to an unlicensed, filthy, drug infested, sober living home. What a joke. We got kicked out of one board and care due to our drug usage and put into a situation that just gave us more and easier access to drugs.

We almost lost our lives in a fire that someone started in the house. We called the police to report the problems in the house and then we were transferred to another one of their homes in Ontario, and finally persuaded the staff to send us to the hospital for a couple of months. It was a relief to get away from that so called sober living home.

Since my girlfriend and I were always getting into trouble together, we each went to a different board and care when we left the hospital. I went to one in West Los Angeles and lasted only four months there before I found myself back in jail. Drinking, using drugs, having promiscuous sex only led me further down that road that really leads nowhere but jail or death. I was taking life for granted and that mindset was catching up with me. After my four month stint in jail, I was sent to a locked medical facility and ultimately was kicked out and landed back in jail for seven more months.

Upon my release, I got excited about going to a board and care up north by the ocean. I thought getting out of the city was going to help me change my attitude towards life. The board and care was pretty nice, clean, and very friendly. Shopping was close by and all was well, for a short time. My drinking became a problem and I ended up in another psychiatric hospital. After a couple of weeks I was released from the hospital and different motels became my home for the next several months.

My new drinking partner became my sex partner and we spent our days doing just that. The drugs and alcohol were becoming a huge problem. I was really getting in deep with the girl and left just in time as her mom started buying me clothes, saying she was investing in me. Whew! Got out of there and off to another board and care I went. This time it was in the Valley. The next stop, prison! When I get out, this time I will make something of myself. I am absolutely through with a life of board and cares, so called sober living homes, psychiatric hospitals, drug dealers, drugs, and alcohol. This is a promise I am making to myself right now!

CHAPTER TWELVE

MORE MOMENTS TO REMEMBER... OR NOT

A S I PAID FOR THE LAST BOX TO BE SHIPPED it finally dawned on me that I would be housing all my mom's dolls along with mine. Wow, I couldn't wait to see how! Too bad that mom couldn't still be around hers. However, her room at the nursing home was just big enough to accommodate her bed, nightstand, lounge chair, dressers, and television.

Part of mom wanted to go to the nursing home because she knew that she needed more care than what she was getting or could get at home. But then there was the part that knew she wouldn't be with her dog anymore, or any of her pretty things. She was a good sport about the whole situation, though, which made the situation much easier on me and my sister.

Oh, I have so many memories of my mom growing up. I thought back once again to the time we lived in the South.

As I reached for the candy bar that I had waited for all day, I heard those words that made my heart stop, "Lady, lady, lady." "Lady your car is rolling down the street." Mom stood there like a deer in the headlights, just frozen.

We were standing in a little bus that served as a neighborhood store,

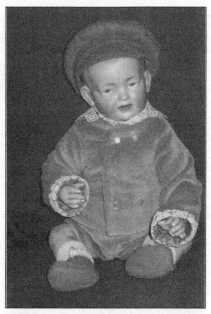

Going to a new home.

since we lived so far from a town. This little bus would drive around and park on different streets during the day to accommodate the families who were not able to get to town.

The streets were lined with fairly deep sandy ditches which meandered up and down through the green belts where row houses were scattered throughout. There were no sidewalks or curbs separating the street from these sandy ditches.

"Lady, don't just stand there." With that, mom stepped outside and screamed as she watched our little car roll down the street, and into the sandy ditch. When I heard her scream, I ran out and saw the rear end of our car sticking up in the air, and its nose stuck in the sand.

Mom had just learned to drive and didn't realize that the emergency brake should be engaged on a hill. Oh, I do remember the conversation in our home that night. It was one of many about mom's driving escapades. The one that was really scary happened in a forest.

I looked up and we were slipping, sliding, and weaving in and out of

Going to a new home.

trees. I had been coloring in the back seat. The last thing I saw, we were driving on a two lane country road. I don't know what happened in those few seconds that I looked down to color. Since I didn't know what was going on, I said nothing. Another reason was there were prayers being said by the lady in the front seat.

We had been at the army base shopping at the Post Exchange (PX) and were on our way back home. Groceries were flying all over the back seat, things were rolling around in the trunk, and all of a sudden a hand pushed me down on the floor. Things got very quiet and the car came to a stop.

I crawled off the floor, climbed onto the seat and looked out the window. There we were in the middle of a forest with the nose of our car right up against a tree. Actually, when we all got out and looked, the car was just inches away from that tree and the ground was completely covered with wet leaves. We all just stood there looking at the tree, then at my mom who was shaking and crying, then back at the tree. The ladies who were in the car with my mom both said, "Good job, you got us through a difficult situation."

Apparently a car was passing another car on the two lane highway we were traveling on, and my mom, being a new driver thought the only way to avoid being hit head on, was to veer off the road. Unfortunately, she didn't realize that she was driving right into the woods. At the end of it all, they all just laughed and hugged each other. That day I came to realize the strength of friendship, and what the power of love could do for someone. My mom had been crying and said she didn't know what to do next. But because of their lack of criticism and their powerful support, she agreed to try to drive us out of the forest. We all climbed back into the car and my mom navigated us, very slowly, I might add, through all the trees back on the road.

Now, here I am in Chicago, once again, creating more memories with mom at the nursing home.

CHAPTER THIRTEEN

CERTIFICATES

A S THE TEACHER HANDED ME MY CERTIFICATE, I felt so proud of myself, for the certificate was in Anger Management. "Shawn you have improved 99%. When you started coming to this class you were an angry young man, full of rage, who acted out inappropriately. You have really applied the tools that you have been taught. I am proud of you." She was right, although I'm sure being clean and sober has something to do with it as well. I sent Joyce all the other certificates that I received and this one will join them. Boy, I feel good. This is the first time I have ever completed anything in a classroom setting, except for that art contest. It is also the first time that I can remember getting kudos and encouragement from a teacher. Funny, it took prison for me to experience this.

I didn't think I would get anything out of the classes and was really reluctant to go. When I realized that going to the classes would get me out of general population and more freedom, I decided to go.

Being part of a group of fifty guys, inmates at that, was kind of intimidating at first. However, I had to get passed that if I wanted to stay. I learned to take deep breaths when I got nervous, or upset. Pretty soon, I was comfortable and when asked questions, was one of the first to answer. Every one clapped when I answered a question correctly, and that made me feel good.

Reading and seeing films about what drugs and alcohol can do to the body, really made an impression on me. Especially seeing what crystal meth can do. Drugs are no joke. When I got my Substance Abuse Certificate, I knew I would never use again. No drugs. No alcohol! I remember writing a letter to Joyce telling her how I felt about the class, and included the certificate. She was so proud of me, and that encouraged me even more to continue to do good things in my life.

My favorite class was the Body Tune-up class. Since I have always liked working out, learning new exercises, new ways to bulk up, and new ways to stay trim really held my interest. I couldn't wait until class ended to try out what I learned. Exercising every day felt good and helped pass the time. Push ups, back, arms, and crunches kept me going. Getting buff was earning respect from other inmates and that felt good.

Boy, Assertiveness Training was really different for me. I always felt that being assertive was being aggressive. When I drank I was really aggressive, starting fights if I didn't get what I wanted. Aggressiveness is what put me here. Now, I get it. Assertiveness is about speaking up for me in a non-violent way. Speaking up for me has always been difficult unless I was drinking. I never felt that I had the right to speak up or to speak my mind. However, as my self-esteem and confidence gets stronger and stronger, hopefully, I will get better at this.

It was exciting to learn more in groups. A far cry from when I was a kid going to school. Being bullied and pushed around was all I knew back then, fighting to prove I was tough, but always losing. I was a pretty boy. The school did nothing to build my self-esteem or confidence, for the teachers made me feel stupid. I don't remember any rewards of any kind for getting answers correct or for good anything. No stars, no candy, no nothing. In my prison classes, candy bars were our reward, and I always got one. Yep, I was doing well!

The freedom that comes from going to the classes is great. My favorite part is going to the canteen and getting food. Soups, chips, instant coffee, candy, chili, and of course, cinnamon rolls. Back in my room I can make coffee by using the hot water from the tap and kick back. Trading and borrowing food is a big thing here. I can loan two soups and get four soups in return. Getting paid back is more of a sure thing here in prison than on the outside. For in here, there are consequences that are quite harsh if someone doesn't keep their word. We are always looking for ways to get more food.

One guy who was always bragging about how he, because he worked out so much, could do flips off the bed. So, I told him I would give him five soups if he could show me. Well, he gave it a good try. He got positioned on the bed, taking his time to get his feet just right. Measured his distance and took a stance. He sure looked like he knew what he was doing. All of a sudden he gave out a yell and went for it. Well, he got off the bed just fine, flipped all right, but landed on his head. I felt so bad, that I gave him the soups anyway. He sure had heart!

The more I thought about my classes, what I've learned, the teacher and the certificate I was holding in my hand, I realized that so much of my life had passed me by while I drank, used and fought. No more. I liked learning. I liked feeling good about myself. I liked participating in life in a more healthy way. I was starting to like me, really like me. I knew that this certificate represented a new beginning.

CHAPTER FOURTEEN

THE REV

P SSST, YOU ARE SPEAKING." "No, I'm not." "Yes, you are, look, here is your name on the program." I am now in panic mode. Invited as a guest to this inner city African American church should not mean that I give a talk, however, sure enough, there was my name about five names down the program list. What was I going to do?

First, I am not prepared; second, this is a very passionate church. A lot of hallelujahs and amens! My lectures are real white bread and these ministers are anything but white bread. As I look further down the program, it became apparent that this was a celebration to include talks from guest ministers, me being one of them. To make matters worse, every speaker upon completion of their short talk played some sort of instrument or sang a song. So not only was I white bread, but I have no artistic talent, unless, one considers playing a comb artistic.

Well, I did take vows as an Interfaith Minister, which means, white bread or not, I will be speaking at the church of alleluias and amens. I thought back to that time at St. John Divine in New York City.

Bells ringing echoed deep within my chest, my heart was pounding as I stood with seventy other people in the largest Gothic Cathedral in the country. We were dressed in our individualized robes, creating a multi-colored rainbow in the middle of the temple. Mine was sea foam green and flowed gracefully around me. Beautiful! Holding our candles, we were all waiting for our ordination to begin. The music started, our cue to begin

I'm official.

One of my ocean weddings.

the procession down the aisle toward the center alters. This was it! Here we go! This was the culmination of our two-year commitment to our interfaith studies at the Seminary. What a journey it had been.

Two by two we walked down the aisle holding our lit candles. The middle of the temple was glowing lighting each one of us like angels. Surreal! What a beautiful scene. As we took our seats, priests and ministers placed sacred texts on an altar before us. Jewish, Christian, Islamic holy books, including Hindu, Buddhist and Zoroastrian texts all sitting side by side. It would be nice if people of different faiths could do the same. There were even a few New Thought books as well!

One of our classmates was a professional singer on Broadway and sang a very emotionally moving song in which he was the voice of God. The song depicted God saying that he heard some of His people cry, was aware of some of His people in pain, and asks who can He send to help His people. We all answered, "It is I Lord, send me." We all interacted with the song answering collectively. I remember the feeling I had during that song and answering with all my heart and soul. That feeling was one of a very deep love for everyone. Words really cannot be used to describe the deepness of this feeling.

Leaving our seats, we created a circle around the altar that held all of the sacred writings. One by one, each clergy blessed us. We were then presented our diplomas with a flower. This serene, yet joyous celebration was definitely one of the highlights of my life.

Founding the Holistic Center had started me on this journey. I knew when I left the corporate world, I would never go back to work in that kind of environment again. I loved being part of something that offered teachings on how to take responsibility for one's own life, medically, emotionally and spiritually. When the Center spawned an Interfaith Fellowship, I knew the seminary was on my agenda. The Interfaith Fellowship became an Interfaith Church.

Those times were definitely challenging. Living off of my savings, running a Holistic Center, going through the Seminary, giving up my home and renting out a couple of rooms in a lady's home for my daughter and I was what I had to do to make ends meet, and even then, it was a struggle. I met my second husband during that time and thought things would become better, and in some ways they did, however, my marriage became

Ordination at St. John Devine.

another challenge in my life.

The morning of my ordination, my husband flew in for the ceremony, had me pick him up from the airport, then left immediately following the ceremony. On the way back from the airport I had mixed feelings about the whole situation. On one hand, I appreciated the effort he made to come in for the ceremony, however, everyone else's family was staying and sharing in the festivities. He was chasing a piece of art. He was always chasing a piece of art. Buying and selling art was his game, above everything else, including his family, which were his daughter and me. After nine years I would think I would be used to doing special things by myself, however, the hurt I felt in my heart was always the same.

As I was reflecting on my ministry, time was ticking away. The last speaker was an Asian minister, who after his talk pulled out a trumpet and played some song on it. Now, this was getting serious.

This situation brought up another memory about a time I was at a memorial service right after I was ordained. Over two hundred people were at the service to pay their respects to a woman who I knew for a brief time. After sitting there for quite some time, her husband announced the minister did not show up. The gal I was with, nudged me and said, "You're a minister, go up there and speak!" Well, my objections were not even acknowledged as she nudged me again and said, "You need to do something." I knew she was right as I got up and walked down the aisle, which seemed like it was never going to end, thinking "Can't wait to see what I'm going to say." I climbed up some stairs, turned around, and started talking. I don't remember much of what I said, however, it must have been just fine, for many, many people came up to me afterwards and thanked me.

Okay, I only have two more speakers in front of me. I have to think, think! I'll go to the bathroom, that's what I'll do. Think, think! As I walked back from the bathroom toward the sanctuary I saw a picture that seemed to jump off the wall towards me. Okay! Now, I know what I am going to say. When my turn came, I confidently stood behind the podium and expounded words of wisdom. Thank goodness for that picture.

One of the men that came with our group was a songwriter and singer, so I invited him up to take his place at the keyboards that were to the left of the stage, and the others from our group gathered around him. We all sang a song that he had written, and that was my musical contribution. I don't think any of them ever forgave me for calling on them without any preparation or notice. However, that was my only choice. So much better than playing a comb.

CHAPTER FIFTEEN

TRAINS, PLANES, AND AUTOMOBILES

I 'M OUT AND IN STOCKTON AT THE TRAIN STATION." Am I dreaming or am I really free? Saying those words to Joyce on the telephone felt so good. When she told me to call her when I got into Los Angeles I got excited. I didn't know where I was or how to get to the Los Angeles station, and was grateful for some guys that showed me the way.

Upon my release, I was very nervous, since I really didn't know where I would end up. I was hoping to live with Joyce; however, we never talked about that. Her response on the phone, when I called her, gave me more hope. The train took me so far, and then I had to transfer to a bus. My heart was beating so fast when the bus pulled into the station. Was I really here? It felt like a dream. Now I had to decide how I would get a hold of Joyce, since I didn't have a phone. I then did the only thing I could think of, which was to walk to the jail. I knew there were always volunteers waiting outside to drive inmates to the mission. So, I couldn't believe I was actually walking toward the jail, the last time I was down in this area, I was walking out of the jail.

I saw this guy sitting in his car. He was waiting for inmates to be released to give them rides, so I asked him if I could borrow his phone. He said he would dial the number for me, and he did. I heard him ask "are you Shawn's mom?" And by the response, she must have said yes. She made a deal with him to drive me all the way to her house, which is not close to where we were. She must have told him she would pay him a lot, for off we went.

Being so nervous, I talked non-stop the whole drive. I am not even sure what I talked about, but I am sure the driver knew my whole life story by the time we got to Joyce's.

I saw Joyce standing out in the driveway type street behind her condo. She looked so beautiful to me. I think I jumped out of the car even before it stopped. I must have looked crazy, hopping out of a rolling car, and holding a plastic bag full of everything I owned. She came over to me, hugged me, and I felt like I was home. I was hoping that my feelings were true.

I can't remember if I took a shower, then or the next morning, for I was so excited just to be somewhere other than prison. The next morning we talked and talked over coffee. Then went and applied for disability benefits. Joyce was all over it. She took me shopping for underwear, shirts, pants and shoes which started our trip off. As we continued through the store, groceries were filling the basket. Joyce was not working, so it looked like I could live with her, which made me feel really happy and grateful.

Well, the next day I needed to check in with the parole office, although I was a day late. The understanding officer worked it out with us. Even though it took a lot of talking, persuading, and several long trips to get my case transferred to Ventura from Pomona, it finally was.

Over the next few days and weeks, we talked, got to know each other on a deeper level developing a close relationship. I was calling her mom, and had been for quite a while through my letters. However, I was really feeling her. I was beginning to really believe I had a mom. She treated me like her son, and her friend, and I felt her love for me.

To stay and be part of this lady's life, I had to stay clean and sober. I was up for that. So, I went to four or five Alcoholics Anonymous meetings a week. In one of the meetings, a man stopped me and asked me if I would like him to be my sponsor. Even though, I really wasn't sure about all this, I agreed. Well, from that moment on, another new journey began.

Meeting with my new sponsor actually felt good. He guided me, helped me with all the assignments, he reviewed my work, called me on my bullshit, and gave me props when deserved. I came to love him a lot.

He really was a lifeline in my life. Now, I had two people I knew I could count on, no matter what. Such a good feeling!

In the midst of all this, my new family and I set off on a trip to Disney World in Florida. Disney World, just hearing that word I felt excitement mixed with some fear. I didn't know where Florida was, I just knew it was very far. How lucky I was to be included in this family-planned trip. I felt so special, so loved, and so accepted. I was not used to the feelings I was having. Feeling special was certainly a new feeling. I have felt loved at different times in my life. However, that love always seemed short lived. Accepted, wow, I can't remember ever feeling accepted, truly accepted for *me*.

We left the house at 4:45 a.m. to get to the bus which was to take us to the airport. Getting up that early was normally very hard for me because of the medicine I take. However, that morning I got some energy that seemed to propel me out of bed. I was apprehensive about the trip, but excited at the same time.

The bus took us almost right to the door of a building that had the name of our airline. We gave our suitcases to men outside the building walked into the building and waited in a line that checked our IDs and then herded us to a conveyor belt where we put things that we were carrying into plastic trays. I even had to take off my shoes. Then each one of us had to walk through a tunnel-like machine. When I walked through the machine, it made a noise. I was informed the metal on my belt sounded off the alarm. I took off my belt, walked through the tunnel once again, and retrieved all my stuff on the other side.

We had to walk quite a ways to where our plane was, and after a brief wait, we boarded our plane. I felt like I was watching a movie. As the plane started to move, then the engines got louder and louder, and we were moving faster and faster, I felt like I was going to take off and fly. When the plane actually lifted off the ground, I could feel myself being pulled back into the seat. The next thing I knew, I was flying. What a thrill!

By the time we landed, it was late afternoon. We got our luggage and walked over to a car rental counter. The next thing I knew, someone drove up in a van and told us that this was our car. We all climbed into the vehicle and headed out of the airport. Wow, what a day! I was in a dreamlike state. It was like I went to sleep in prison and woke up in the middle of my dream. The last thing I remember was pulling up in front of Joyce's condo holding a bag of clothing, and now here I am in another state.

CHAPTER SIXTEEN

"IT'S ME, SHAWN"

TRYING TO DECIDE WHICH DOG TO CHOOSE was becoming an almost impossible task, when my thoughts were interrupted by an incoming call from a telephone number that I did not recognize. Normally I wouldn't have answered a call from a number that I didn't know, but something told me that this call was important, so I pushed the answer button and said "This is Joyce." "Hi, it's me, Shawn," was the reply. "I'm out. I'm in Stockton."

My mind was not prepared for that message. I had, after much deliberation with myself, decided that I would get a dog so my grandson would have the experience of being raised with a dog. My daughter and her husband had jobs that didn't allow them to have a dog. My last fur person passed away just two years ago and I had vowed not to tie myself down with the responsibility of another pet. So, here I sit at the dog pound with two of the cutest dogs ever. Shawn's call interrupted my decision-making process, so I gave the dogs back to the handlers and left the caged yard.

Shawn had been sentenced to six years in prison for agreeing to some sort of deal that I never really understood. However, I still thought that was too harsh of a punishment based on his original offense of the $14 ordeal. Our judicial system doesn't always work in a justifiable manner. He committed his crime eight years earlier, when he threatened a guy at the board and care for $14. He was turned in by the manager, and served four months of a one year sentence. That is when he was put on three years of probation. During the next couple of years, he went to several facilities. None of them really worked, since he was using drugs and drinking heavily. I am sure that checking in with his probation officer was the farthest thing from his mind. The court made some sort of deal with Shawn. He would go back to prison, if he violated the law in any way. He was off his medication at the time of the offer, and really never understood what the court was saying. Our system is not set up for people who have a mental illness and that is really too bad. Our jails have become institutions for the mentally ill. So, when Shawn was caught up in a fight at his last board and care, the records showed that he was in violation of probation. Because of the earlier deal he had made with the court, off to prison he went.

Once again, I received a call right before Christmas telling me that Shawn was arrested. My heart just sank when I heard that news. I didn't hear from Shawn for quite a while, however, when I did, I was glad that

My new home with my new dog.

he reached out even though it was only through a letter and not a call. We wrote back and forth for the entire four and half years. At first I was very worried about Shawn, however, over time his letters became more positive and they started containing certificates from classes that he was attending.

Okay, now, another call. This time a release call. So, now what? I really didn't know. I didn't know if I was to meet him downtown. I didn't know what time. I didn't know where. I didn't know a whole lot of stuff. Another call came late that night.

"Do you know Shawn Hall?"

"Yes," I replied.

"He wants to talk with you."

"Hi, it's me, Shawn. I'm here in front of the county jails. Can you come get me?"

"Of course, can you put the other person back on the phone?"

My mind was going a mile a minute. Driving to where he was at this time of night was not such a good idea. I was thinking about the next step I would take when I heard, "Hello, where do you live?" I told the voice on the other end of the phone and told him that I could pay him if he were willing to drive Shawn to my home. We agreed on a price, I gave him directions, and waited for their arrival.

The car pulled up and both Shawn and the driver got out. I found out that the driver was a volunteer who took inmates who were released from the county jail to different missions in town. I was so grateful to him that I not only paid him what we agreed upon, but gave him a hefty tip as well.

As the car pulled away, Shawn stood there, in the street, holding a plastic bag that contained his meager belongings. He looked so tired. Although I shared in his joy of being free, my heart felt heavy for even though I could not really know all that he had been through, I felt some of his pain. I made the decision right then and there, that he no longer would live in another board and care. He was now going to share my home with me. That decision changed both of our lives.

CHAPTER SEVENTEEN

THE HAPPIEST PLACE ON EARTH

T HERE IT IS!" "WOW, HOW BEAUTIFUL." I was a bit confused, but finally realized they were talking about where we were going to be staying. "It is such a big hotel!" "This really isn't a hotel; it is what is called a resort." We will be staying at a resort." Well, whatever it was called, it was a beautiful place.

We had a huge kitchen, dining room, a living room, a sitting room, a huge master bedroom with a sunken tub, and a patio. I had never seen anything like this. "It's so big. After we carried our suitcases in, we all went to the pool. "Boy, it's hot." "Yes, Florida stays warm into the evening unlike California." I have never really liked the hot weather and here I was in what felt like an oven. I even went into the pool a little while even though my shyness and anxiety were running high. Both usually keep me out of crowds and the pools. And there were a lot of people in the pool area.

Afterwards, Julie and Joyce went to the store to stock up on breakfast food for the week. When they came back, we all just crashed. Joyce's daughter and her family had the master bedroom, Joyce had the little den area, and I had the living room. I never wanted to wake up from this dream.

After sleeping in a little the next morning, eating our cereal, eggs, bagels and juice, off we went to the Wild Animal Kingdom, one of Disney World's parks. Animals of all kinds, shapes, and sizes were in the park. The trees and even the rocks were carvings of different animals. I could have been in the jungles of Africa, for there were even lions and elephants.

There was a carnival-like area within the park with all kinds of games to play for stuffed animals. Playing one of the games, I won a stuffed turtle for Joyce's granddaughter and a little lion for Joyce. Boy, I sure felt proud of myself. I wanted to yell, "I got game." It felt good to feel that way, for it had been a long time since I had. Even though it was so very hot and I was complaining a lot about the heat, I was having a really good time.

The Magic Kingdom was the next day's agenda. Joyce's grandson started our adventure by climbing up to a tree house. A house built way up in a tree. I guess it could work as long as it didn't rain.

Next, we all climbed into a boat that took us into the land of pirates. We were in the middle of two ships firing cannons at each other and ended up in a town that was being taken over by pirates. I have to say, those pirates really looked real for I could see the hair on the pirates' legs. Now it can't get any more real than that.

A mansion that was haunted in Louisiana was where we picked up ghost hitchhikers and laughing on a roller coaster felt so good. I hadn't laughed like that for such a very long time.

I climbed into a flying elephant with Joyce's grandson, took off next on another roller coaster that propelled us fast up into space. So fun! Train rides, water rides, race cars and even the merry-go-round. My emotions were spinning as fast as some of the rides, for I was sure this was a dream.

Hot and tired we all drag ourselves back to our resort. While Joyce and her family played in the pool I just hung out on one of the lounge chairs. I had to clear my head since it was a kaleidoscope of thoughts. My feelings were all over the place. Happy, excited, fearful, worrisome. The day had been great; however, I was emotionally and physically exhausted. I was glad to be relaxing since I knew that the next day was going to be another exciting and full day.

Seeing all the arcade games overwhelmed me. Here I was, in a three-story building just full of every arcade game one could dream of. I was suddenly ten years old again and just went for it. I played all the games I could possibly play. Smashing and killing aliens, bowling, shooting gangsters, and stopping zombies were some of my exercises for the day. The air was cool from the air conditioner and a relief from the triple digit degree

The happiest place on earth.

A big hand to welcome us to the Wild Animal Kingdom.

heat of the outdoors. What fun I had. Three floors of games kept me busy for the whole day. We ended the day with another quick dip in the pool, dinner and then crashed early to be prepared for the following day at Epcot, which I understood was another theme park. My head felt like one of those snow globes.

One minute I was in France eating delicious pastry, the next minute I was in Norway watching a movie about the Vikings. Those Vikings were something else again. They were pirates who wore horned helmets. I liked learning this way much better than any school. Epcot was really something.

Finding pearls in oysters was a new one for me. I didn't know that was where pearls came from. I picked out an oyster for Joyce and it turned out to be a blue/black pearl, a very rare color I was told. Everyone else was picking white ones. I felt really special, just like the pearl I picked.

We visited so many pretend countries each with their own culture and food. We watched a Mariachi band and ate Mexican food overlooking the water. It was a nice day, hot, but nice. I never thought I would ever be experiencing anything like this. I didn't even know things like this existed. I hated to leave and hoped that we could come back here someday.

We stopped for lunch on the way to see Joyce's dad and I met her aunt and uncle. They were very nice people and seemed to accept me without judgment. I was a little uncomfortable and needed to step outside the restaurant to get my bearings. After a couple of cigarettes I was good.

We ate and visited for a little over an hour, and then we were back on the road again. Got to our hotel early enough to go see Joyce's dad and then out for dinner. I loved the hotel, small, but I had my own room with Joyce's grandson. We had two double beds, a kitchenette, and a nice bathroom. So cool! The hotel was on the beach and had its own swimming pool as well as a little garden patio where I could smoke. I thought this must be heaven.

Our evening turned out to be a real wet one. We went out for dinner at a hole in the wall kind of place. Part of the restaurant was on a pier, where we sat. While we were eating, it started to rain, slow at first, then it got torrential. We were just starting to eat our dinner when the rain began. Even though we were under a table umbrella, we were drenched. We just sat there in the rain when all of a sudden the power went out on the pier.

We gathered up the kids and ran for our lives into the bar, which was also dark. There we were, drenched and in the dark. I sat outside not thinking it was so funny, but Joyce and her daughter kept laughing and saying, "It is just another fun adventure." It takes me awhile to roll with those kinds of punches, since I have a tendency to start complaining about things like that. There I sat, smoking and looking through the sheets of rain into the darkness. To me, it was kind of eerie! I tried hard to find the humor in sitting in the pouring rain while eating my Philly cheesesteak sandwich in the dark. I just couldn't get there! Soaking wet, we made our way back to the van and to our hotel. Yeah! Dry, full, and happy, we all just sat around and laughed about the evening, and I did too.

Chicago was less hectic as we stayed at the apartment of Joyce's sister and visited her mom every day at a nursing home. Joyce and I took a bus every morning to the nursing home and stayed all day, then went back to the apartment for dinner. I enjoyed my time there and met the rest of her family. Unlike mine, her family was small. It consisted of her mom, sister, brother-in-law, niece, her husband and her cousin, all of whom I met in Chicago. Joyce's ex-husband came over to the apartment to meet me and I really liked him. I saw him again at Christmas when he came to visit.

Joyce and I flew home from Chicago alone and even though I had a great time, it was good to get back. It was nice to have a home to come back to. That felt good!

CHAPTER EIGHTEEN

BOBS

H OLD ON, HERE COMES ANOTHER TURN." Wow, what fun I was having at this theme park riding all the rides with my family, including the newest member, Shawn. The weather was hot, however, even though we were all melting a bit, our laughter kept us from complaining too much. We all just enjoyed being with each other and celebrating the fact that Shawn was with us.

As I climbed into the seat of another roller coaster, I thought back to a time in my life when a roller coaster did get the best of me.

The thrill of that first hill was breathtaking! The car took us up to the top of what looked like the end of the earth, and plunged us down, around a curve and then dove straight into a dark tunnel. Wow, no wonder it was called the Fireball. It was one of five wooden roller coasters at Riverview, which was the largest privately-owned amusement park in our country at the time.

I loved going there as a child, with its music, the noise, which was a mixture of the screams from the rides, the calls from the barkers to "come on in and try your luck" and the curious that gathered around the side show. The tattooed woman always fascinated me. It had taken me a while to get she wasn't born that way, that she had deliberately chosen to be stuck with needles that injected dye into her skin just to get those pictures that covered her whole body. Did she do it to be in the side show, I wondered? If not, then why? She never said and I never figured it out.

The Bobs Wooden Roller Coaster.

The Fun House at Riverview.

Monkeys, wearing different colored vests sitting on matching motor-ized cars, were waiting anxiously for the sound of the gun to start their race. Bang! They're off and the air was filled with the cheers from the crowd and a deep voice announcing the race as if it were the Kentucky Derby. The monkey that finished all his laps and crossed the finish line rang the bell indicating he was the winner. While people who placed their bets on that monkey were collecting their winnings, the monkeys took their places back on top of their cars, received a treat, and waited once more for the sound that started their race.

Then there was the "Bobs." It boasted being the fastest wooden roller coaster in the world. I remember the time I went on it 13 times in a row. For a nickel, you could ride again and again and again. You could ride it as many times as you could stand being thrown around and jostled.

Now this old time amusement park with all the carnies yelling out, "Come on in and try your luck." It was a place where sailors from a nearby base would come, have fun and meet gals, all hoping for their *luck* in the Tunnel of Love.

I would have kept riding that coaster to break my record of 18 times, however, I hit my head on the side of the car cutting my ear. I didn't know it was bleeding until we started down one of the steepest hills and saw the blood from my ear being blown behind me on to a sailor's nice clean white uniform. Needless to say, when the ride ended, I got off as quickly as possible. I am sure that sailor never knew what happened as he looked at his bloodstained uniform. He may still be scratching his head. Who knows?

CHAPTER NINETEEN

AMENDS

I WAS CHANGING IN A GOOD WAY! I was growing emotionally, and it felt good! There were times I really did not want to do the work that my sponsor assigned. However, when I did it, I felt good inside. Taking a personal inventory of myself was a little painful, however, it pushed me further along on my journey of emotional healing. Making amends to people that I had harmed in some way was scary. The first place I went to make amends was at the last board and care that I had lived in. That felt good. I looked good; new clothes, all coordinated with my new shoes. It was the new Shawn. I was actually strutting around the board and care, not really wanting to show off, well, that is not true, I did want to show off a bit. Afterwards, Joyce and I went to the pizza place that we used to go to when she came to visit me. This time was different, because I was different. Afterwards, we kept with tradition and shopped at the 99-cent store.

The next place I went to make amends was to the board and care in Compton. I was very nervous to go back into that area since that area holds lots of bad memories for me. Geographically the energy there was very unsettling to my psyche. I thought that I would just make the amends and leave quickly. However, I pushed myself to stay and visit some places that were part of my childhood. This included the swap meet that I had spent many a day at when I was a kid; even bought myself a jacket.

We then went to the group home where I lived when my mom passed away. No one was there that I knew, however, just looking around brought back so many memories. I looked around, went into the different rooms, and talked with the lady that was there. I pictured myself hanging out, like I used to do, and overwhelming feelings just ran through me, like the shivers. Eventually, I was able to find the wonderful loving lady who ran the group home at that time, and I made amends at her home. She was the lady who taught me manners, respect, and tried to teach me religion. She sent me and personally paid for that private Christian school. She greeted me with a smile and a hug, and said prayers with me after making my amends with her.

On the way home and all that evening, I reflected on the day. I was so happy to be where I was and was willing to let the past be the past. It is true; you cannot go back for it is not the same.

Making amends to the police department wasn't as hard as I had expected it to be. There I was, standing in front of three police officers making my amends. They were so gracious and listened very attentively and accepted my apology. I could tell they were impressed with my willingness to be vulnerable.

My brothers were always on my mind. I was hoping they were okay. Joyce kept looking for them and the rest of my family as well. One day, she got a clue as to where they might be. We tried calling all the numbers that she found, however, they were all disconnected. We did not know if the addresses that we found were any good. She suggested I write some letters, hoping one would find its way to a sister or brother. And one did!

CHAPTER TWENTY

COMING HOME AFTER QUITE A WHIRLWIND TRIP with my daughter, her husband, my grandchildren, and Shawn I was greeted with a phone call from the lady that was renting from my husband. "I know that you really aren't together anymore, but Don needs help; he is having much more trouble walking these days. Would you be willing to help him?" "Of course" and off I went.

As I drove to his big home in the hills of Westlake Village I thought about all the times that I had made the same drive, for oh so many reasons. My twenty-one-year relationship with Don has been one of many challenges. Although Don is a good man and can really connect with animals and small children, emotional relationships with adults are very difficult for him. That is the place where most of our challenges have stemmed from. Another place is when Don felt like his space, personal or physical, was being invaded; he became sarcastic and combative.

Even though Don and I were married, he was unable to share his home with me. The master bedroom was huge and so was the walk-in closet. It was set up for him, and that did not change when I married him nine years ago. The walk-in closet was a game room. It held several coin operated machines, including a pinball machine, slot machines, and one of those machines where one tries to grab a toy or a piece of candy with a movable claw. The second closet was for his clothes. Therefore, my clothes hung on the other side of the house in one of the small bedrooms. This separation represented our relationship and marriage.

I had agreed to live with Don five years into our relationship, and left after nine months very angry. We had gone to counseling and the counselors basically threw up their hands in frustration. Don did not get the concept of sharing, even though he invited me to share his life with him. When I left, I did not see Don for almost a year. Don came back into my life with a mouthful of "I'm sorry and a pocketful of promises." Later I realized that he missed me all right; he really missed all my help with his business, especially at the shows. However, I didn't realize that until I once again lived with him many years later. This time when I left, I wasn't angry since I realized that Don could not share his home with anyone, not even his daughter whom he had on the weekends. I believe he tried as best he could. So, even though I left, I continued in the relationship for several more years. Then, once again, I had enough.

Helping my daughter plan her wedding and celebrating all the events surrounding it and being free of being belittled, criticized and yelled at was so wonderful. Interestingly, I never missed Don in any way. My daughter had invited Don to her wedding, since she practically grew up with him and his daughter was in her wedding party. I knew that might prove to be uncomfortable, and I was right.

During the reception, he followed me around, asking me to go out for dinner with him. I kept trying to get away from him, however, when I couldn't, I just said simply, "No, I do not want to have dinner with you." I had to do that several times throughout the evening. Finally, he stopped bothering me and I continued to enjoy the celebration.

Being back at work seemed like such a drag after all the hoopla of the wedding celebration. I was trying to get it together and prepare for the work day when I looked up and there was Don. He was wearing a big Sombrero hat, the black velvet kind with all the cheap looking gold threading and tassels. He had gotten down on one knee, balancing the sombrero on his head, his hands placed over his heart, he started to sing, "Be my love, for there is no other…"

When he got back up, he once again asked me to please go to dinner with him. I agreed to have dinner with the understanding that it probably would not go any further than that, for I was enjoying being free of his surly ways.

Dinner was fine; he ordered some fine wine, which surprised me since he did not drink. He had given up drinking due to his divorce and custody battle, however, his daughter had turned 21 during the time we were separated, so he started to have wine with dinner. The conversation went something like, "I am a changed man. I take responsibility for many of the troubles in our relationship. I am willing to share my life and my home with you, if you would please reconsider and be my wife." I remember thinking, "Whoa, where did that come from?"

The next day I flew into Mazatlán, Mexico to meet a friend at her timeshare. She was leaving and I was staying for the remainder of the reservation. My time there was so much fun, filled with adventures in the mountains and the ruins, eating some of the most delicious food and experiencing the Mexican celebration of their independence. All the while, I was thinking about that dinner with Don and the conversation that we had.

I loved feeling free and very independent, once again. Here I had just flown to Mexico, by myself, staying on the coast and not in the rural area, taking busses in the city, and even ventured to the celebration downtown late one evening. Of course, I was one of a very few gringos there and didn't understand what was being said over the speaker that was mounted on one of the buildings. There had to be several hundred people all in the square celebrating by drinking and yelling *Viva Mexico!* So much fun, however, by the time the celebration was over, there were no more busses to take me back to my resort. So there I was wondering what to do next. Of course, open air taxi! I found one and convinced him to take me after he kept saying, "No, too far," but money does talk. So, as I rode in the front of the open air taxi, taking in all the night air again, my thoughts had gone back to the conversation with Don.

Well, here I am. As I pulled into his driveway, Don saw me and smiled.

CHAPTER TWENTY-ONE

REUNITED

TWENTY-TWO MISSED CALLS. What? Twenty-two numbers on my phone. At first I thought they were wrong numbers or just a mistake. I called one of the numbers that appeared on my screen and when the voice on the other end said hello, I knew I was talking to my sister. My heart pounded with excitement as we talked. The calls kept coming in, one right after another. One sister, then another, then another, a brother, and then I talked to Chris and felt such a sense of relief for now I knew he was safe.

The next day we went to see some of my sisters. As we drove through an area that I once was part of, feelings of fear, confusion, sadness coupled with anxiousness and excitement came over me. I had feelings I couldn't even identify. As we drove down my sister's street, my heart pounded in anticipation, then there she was standing in her yard waving. I jumped out and we hugged and hugged. By the time Joyce parked the car, I was already standing with my sister and her husband. When Joyce joined us, we went inside, sat down, and just began talking about the past. Pictures of my nieces and nephews appeared on the table, and then the most amazing thing happened. My sister came out with a picture of my dad, a dad that I never knew. He was an entertainer and lead singer in a 1960s Do Wop group. I'm not sure what I felt, it just seemed so surreal. Here I was, sitting in my sister's kitchen, looking at pictures of family members that I had either never met, or not seen since I was a child.

Mark Jason Hall

My sister, Joyce, and I left to visit another sister at the beauty shop where she was working. We parked, got out, and walked into a little shop and there she was. A beautiful woman whom I had not seen for over 15 years stood looking at me with such love in her eyes. She came over to me and started hugging and kissing me. Tears were in her eyes as well as in mine. It all seemed so unreal. She kept saying "thank you" and "bless you" to Joyce and kept saying "I can't believe it, I can't believe it." I told her that I was clean and sober for almost five years and that I have a sponsor and that I go to meetings. She relayed to us that she had overdosed on pain pills and died, but was revived and knew that it was her second chance at life. "Shawn, this is your second chance," she said. "Keep calling your sponsor and going to your meetings." Every time someone came into the beauty shop she would jump off the couch that we were sitting on and say "this is my baby brother." She was so excited and I was too. As we all walked outside to say goodbye, happiness, and joy filled me up so much that I thought I was going to bust. There I was, standing on the street talking to two of my sisters. Couldn't believe it! Again, it didn't feel real.

I said goodbye and off we went to visit my next sister who was working at the government building. As we drove through the neighborhoods, my sister pointed to a church that our mom used to take us to get money for food. She also pointed out the street where our little house was. Not really sure how I felt at that moment, for I do remember that we had gotten evicted from that house. We pulled up to the government building's parking lot, however, it was locked. So, we parked the car on the street, called my sister and she said she would meet us outside. As we were waiting for her to come out, a police car had someone pulled over down the street, which brought back memories that I would like to forget. Memories of those constant eerie sirens just gave me chills.

There she was walking across the parking lot wearing a dress and heels, looking so pretty. As she got closer, I could see she had tears streaming down her cheeks. She opened the gate, we gravitated to each other with arms wide open, we hugged and hugged, and she kissed me and kissed me. I felt so happy. I actually don't know all the feelings I had, but I know that happiness was one of them. There we all stood on the sidewalk, talking, hugging, kissing and just plain loving on each other. All of a sudden, she went over to Joyce, hugged her, buried her head on her shoulder and sobbed and sobbed. Through her sobs, I could hear the words, thank you, thank you, which she said over and over to Joyce. Joyce started to cry, I had tears in my eyes, and so did my other sister. What a heartfelt and touching scene. I felt like I was in a movie, watching people on a screen, for it just didn't seem real, yet I knew it was.

We continued our journey to see another sister who lived just a few minutes away. There she was walking down the street, we pulled up next to her, and she saw me, smiled, and jumped into the back seat where I was. She had been on her way to the store. She started to sing a song my mom used to sing, and I joined in. Wow, there I was, sitting with the sister that looks like mom, singing a song of the past.

Walking up the stairs to my sister's apartment, my heart was pounding, and I'm sure that the smile was still on my face. My smile felt like it was frozen in place. Look at all those pictures! Pictures of my family, aunts, uncles, nieces, nephew, cousins, all of whom I had never met were taped to the wall above the couch. Wow, I had over 30 nieces and nephews! Surreal!

The fixings for tacos were on the table where a young man was standing getting ready to make one. A little baby was in a walker, and long-haired man came over and introduced himself. He was my sister's boyfriend. The baby was my niece's. My sister got custody of the baby since her daughter was in prison. Her name was Heaven. How appropriate, Heaven, for that is where I felt I was.

We visited for a short while, making small talk, for we were both overwhelmed with the situation. As I was playing with Heaven, there was a knock on the door. I noticed when my sister answered the door there was someone wanting to buy cigarettes. She told them to wait, closed the door, went in the other room, and came back with what they wanted. She had a little hustle going on.

Hugging and saying bye for now, felt so good, for I knew we were back in each other's life. As we drove off, I could see her waving, and there was something so comforting about that. After dropping off my other sister back at her house, we continued our journey back home. What a day! Was it real?

Over time and with Joyce's help, I was able to locate all of my brothers and sisters! I was so happy and relieved to locate them all. I had learned while I was at one of the board and cares that my brother, Mark, had been shot and killed. He was simply in the wrong place at the wrong time. We lived in constant fear that this could happen to any one of us. I was so upset by all of this. I did learn that his killer was convicted for his death. I was deeply saddened about my brother's death and that my family did not know how to reach me to tell me. I was not there for his funeral. When I finally located my younger brother, my heart was filled with joy. He was the last missing piece.

CHAPTER TWENTY-TWO

RESISTANCE

I 'VE MISSED YOU. HOW WAS YOUR TRIP?" "Good, had a lot of fun. It was nice seeing my dad and my aunt and uncle." We did the small talk for a little while, and then we got down to the real talk. I had not seen Don for the last couple of months due to his abusive behavior. Even though I was well aware that he had mild dementia his abusiveness was nothing new, for his personality was just being exasperated with this new development.

"I understand that your walking has become more difficult lately. Is that true?" "Yeah, but I just go slow." "Can I see you walk down the hall?" As I watched Don walk down the hall, my heart went out to him. His gait was so off. He staggered and wobbled. However, he did manage to continue to make it to the end. It was frightening to watch him for fear he would fall, as he had done in the past.

One day the phone rang, I answered it and heard, "Joyce, can you please come and help me since I fell and have been lying on the floor for hours?" When I arrived at his house, there he was on the floor of his bedroom. He had fallen in the hallway and it took him hours to crawl to the bedroom to get to his phone. After several incidents like that, I decided to get monitors for his house. The lady that rented the granny flat was willing to have the base monitor in her place and ultimately became one of his caretakers.

When Don wanted something the charming salesman would come out and he would become very persuasive. Here he was once again, being that charmer. I knew this side of Don very well. He had always been about Don and really did not care too much what I or anyone else was interested in. He used his charm to manipulate the person or situation. As I stood in his kitchen and continued to watch him get himself a cup of coffee, I thought back to the times when he was vibrant, full of energy, and even genuinely kind.

On our first trip to Santa Fe we stopped at the Acoma Indian Pueblo, called the Sky City since it was on top of a mesa. Although we took a bus up to the top, we did walk down the tiny path over and around all the rocks on the steep path down. Don just negotiated the path like he was walking down a sidewalk, where I on the other hand was taking it really slow for fear of toppling all the way down the mesa. That visit happened to turn out to be a very poignant one. It was one of the times that Don wanted to share something with me that I had not experienced before. Something very special happened on top of the mesa.

As we were walking around the top of the mesa Native people were putting out some of the pottery that they had made for sale. Acoma pottery has some interesting designs and colors, including their famous parrot design. All of a sudden, there was something that caught both of our attention. A large coffee mug, not typical of Acoma pottery, was sitting all by itself on a small broken down table. It was made by the Native lady who had just placed the mug outside her door. We walked over to the table, picked up the mug and looked at each other with a combination of amazement and confusion, for it had a name on the mug, mine. Very clear, JOYCE. My name was on this mug. It surely was a sign. I always took it to be a sign that Don and I were meant to be together. Not sure that turned out to be a correct assumption. The lady said that someone had asked her to make a coffee cup with theses colors and designs and to include the name, but never came to pick it up. So, it became mine. It was meant to be mine. I still have that coffee mug displayed in a very special place as a reminder of better times for Don and I.

"I don't think you should be driving. Would you be willing to let me take you where you need to go?" "I'm okay when I sit down. My legs work just fine then. It is only when I walk that I have trouble." "Hmm," I thought, "Let me try it a different way." "Why don't you let me take you to your doctor appointments, and to the hospital for your treatments? This

Top of the Acoma Pueblo, Sky City

The JOYCE coffee mug, Acoma Pueblo.

way, you don't have to park the car and walk all the way into each building." This worked, and he agreed. He was getting infusions at the hospital twice a week and each appointment took up to four to five hours. That was the beginning of my new daily routine.

I was so grateful for the help of the lady that rented from him and from Shawn. Don did not have a good relationship with his daughter for they argued most of the time. As a result, she chose not to participate in his care. There were times Shawn had to lift him into his bed, because he became so weak. Then there were those times where he was walking like he didn't have a problem. However, as the dementia became worse and worse, the doctor's appointments became battlegrounds for he would not listen nor agree with what the doctor was saying or prescribing.

How did it come to this? It seemed that over the last six years I was taking care of a husband who couldn't share his home, money, or life with me. One year after we were married, he broke his neck and during the healing process, he became so abusive that I moved out and lived with my daughter for a while. However, since he really had no one to assist him, I helped him get back on his feet, which took another year. Then, six to eight months later, he was diagnosed with a chronic nerve disease. I remembered how he begged me to marry him and made all sorts of promises. He'll sell his house and together we would purchase a home on the lake. He would make sure that if something happened to him that I would be taken care of and he would travel with me. None of that was coming true. After we were married, he changed his mind about selling his house, never signed or executed the trust he said he had set up for me and we have not traveled together. Well, I guess technically that is not true, we have taken several cruises, which I ultimately ended up alone on since he slept all day.

"Would you like to go out to eat?" "Sure," I said. "I'll drive." As we walked toward my car, I watched with sadness, someone who was once robust and now was just a shell of the man he once was. My eyes filled with tears as he struggled to make it to the car. Don made it, got in, and just said, "Thank you."

CHAPTER TWENTY-THREE

OH SO MUCH MUD!

I SPENT THE NEXT COUPLE OF WEEKS talking to everyone on the phone. That felt so good. I was talking to my family, my sisters, and brothers. Happiness and joy filled me up. Then came the moments of sadness. Some of them were not doing so well. Struggling financially was the biggest issue. Some had health problems that were not being addressed, probably due to money. Worry and sadness started to replace my feelings of happiness and joy.

Busyness with Thanksgiving and shopping for families on the Navajo reservation took my mind off some of my worry thoughts. We had a list of families with names and sizes of each member and there we were looking for outfits. Our cart was filling up with sweaters, blouses, pants, and socks. I kept being sidetracked looking at sweaters, pants, and shirts for myself. We were at a discount store and compared to other stores I have been in, the prices seemed much lower. I started wanting everything. Running from a rack of sweaters to the rack of jackets to the rack of shirts, finally I got hold of myself and went back to look at outfits for the Navajo families that we were going to visit.

Lots of wrapping took place in our house. There was tape and Christmas paper all over. Once the wrapping and packaging were finished, we loaded up the rented van and we were set to go.

Our car was at the car dealer for repair of a seatbelt that our little Chihuahua dog chewed up. We had dropped the car off, rented the van and was preparing to hit the hay early so we could get an early morning start. All of a sudden, we realized that we didn't have our car charger for the phone. We jumped into the loaded van and jetted to the car dealership. Our car was locked up on the roof and there I was jumping over the locked gate, which I had done many times before, however, this time no one was chasing me. Jumping back over the gate, holding the car charger, I felt like a hero that saved the day, or in this case, the night. We were now set to go.

I was excited to be going and be part of something bigger than me. Part of my sobriety and program is being of service to someone else. I was helping Joyce and I knew we would be helping many families. I slept for a couple of hours and woke up at the famous Bagdad Café for breakfast. Cool! I had watched the movie with Joyce and here we were eating at the very same place that was in the movie.

Sitting outside smoking and talking to my sister on the phone, I accidentally burned the top of my new jacket. Man, I was so pissed! I obsessed about it so much that I kept trying to pull out the burnt fur and I just made a hole in the hood. Now I was really pissed. I love this jacket and clothes are so important to me that I was just beside myself. I talked about the jacket for the next two hours. Okay, then I got myself under control, and able to let it go.

I realized that my smoking was getting out of hand. I was smoking more and more and I had burned a pair of my pants and now my jacket. I wanted to quit, didn't want to quit, knew I needed to, but still just wasn't ready to. I started to think back when I had pneumonia and knew I was headed down that road again or something worse if I didn't get the smoking under control. I pushed that back in my mind and decided I would deal with that issue later.

Working out with Joyce, eating healthy and having a good schedule in my life were good healthy choices. I stayed with that thought and gave myself credit for how far I had come from drinking, drugging, and fighting. I am reminded of those days when I look at some of the damage that all those vices caused. Punching a window with my fist when I was drunk almost caused me to lose my finger. That scar, as well as others on my body

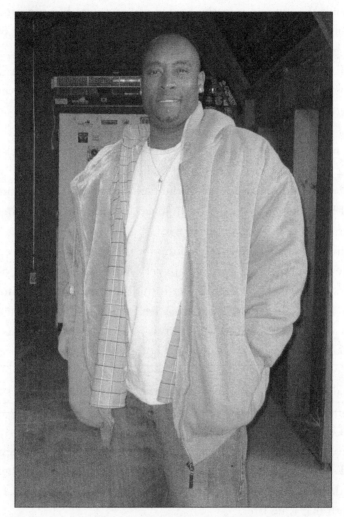

This is the jacket I obsessed about.

is a constant reminder of my past. I gave myself some self-deserved kudos and let go of the smoking issue.

I loved just hanging out in the car with Joyce, just chillin' and listening to music. The mountains were so beautiful since they had just a touch of snow left on them from some recent storm. Happiness, contentedness, and joy filled my being. We stopped along the way just long enough for gas and a bathroom break, so we made it to our destination just before dark.

Checked into the motel, I kicked back and Joyce went to the bazaar to meet her Navajo lady friends. I loved being in the hotel. It gave me a sense of freedom and space. However, sleeping in the bed next to Joyce brought up my feelings and attraction to her as a woman and not just the lady that helped me. The urge to slide in next to her was so great, that I had a hard time falling asleep. I pushed the feeling aside and the next morning we drove the 50 miles to deliver the gifts to the families. We met Joyce's friend, Sylvia, who helped us organize our packages at what the Navajo's call, the Chapter House, which is a meeting place. I pumped up basketballs, sorted clothing by sizes, and helped carry the heavy packages. One by one, the families started coming to pick up their gifts. Many extra gifts sat all in a row on separate tables as we were expecting more kids to show up. Apparently, the roads were so muddy that many of the families couldn't get out of their roads. Therefore, we ended up with some of those extra gifts. So, Joyce made bags for her three lady friend's families and one for me as well. The one she made for me we ultimately sorted and were able to give my family some of those gifts. I felt excited about this and could not wait to get home to pass them out. We decided to leave the reservation the next day since we couldn't get to the home we were to stay in due to the muddy roads. The night before Joyce pushed me to go to the bizarre with her, however, I had a slight panic attack, left and was annoyed because I didn't want to go in the first place. I went because Joyce wanted me to and I did not want to let her down. Once again, thoughts of Joyce crept into my head. I hung onto those thoughts and let them put me to sleep.

CHAPTER TWENTY-FOUR

PILLS, PILLS AND MORE PILLS

W ELL, THE LAST COUPLE OF MONTHS certainly have been interesting. Interesting is a word I use when I really don't know how to accurately describe something. Kind of like when someone uses that word to describe your blind date.

Finding Shawn's family has generated a lot of phone calls for Shawn as well as a lot of excitement. Just this last month, we found his last remaining family member, his youngest brother. He was in a local jail for crossing the state line to see his baby mama. That was a violation of his probation, which he was on. Shawn felt complete now. for he found all of his family members and I felt complete seeing him so happy.

As happy as Shawn was, Don was not. I had to call the show producers of several shows in New Mexico to cancel Don's reservations. So sad! He started the antique shows more than 25 years ago and he is an icon in the business. People in the Native American antique business know him as well as many galleries in Santa Fe, New Mexico since he is respected for his knowledge in this area. Don's walking had become so unstable over the last several months that even if I had driven him to Santa Fe, he would not have been able to take the grueling days that followed. He loved the business and loved to impart his knowledge to anyone who would listen as they walked by his booth, however, along with the enjoyment of that, it was very tiring. Since Don argued with me about everything these days I was surprised when he did not put up a fuss when I called and cancelled. He just knew it was the right thing to do. I felt so sad for him.

By now he was on a plethora of pills. Along with the pills, he gave himself an injection of vitamins every day, and was still going to the hospital for infusions. The hospital became his social outlet. He knew every nurse and aid as well as many of the patients. They would play practical jokes on each other, talk about their families and Don would educate everyone in Native American Indian art. He would bring gifts for everyone, little tchotchkes that he had collected along his travels. Of course, everyone got one of his famous two dollar bills. He called it a "nice person" award. When he handed someone a two dollar bill, he would say, "You won the nice person award today." He told the recipient to put it behind their driver's license and that way they would never be broke. It was a nice gesture and people did what he told them to do, putting it behind their driver's license. Waiters would come up to us and show Don that they still had the two dollar bill that he had given them sometime in the past.

There were pills all over the place. Pills on the counter, pills on the floor, pills on chairs, pills all over. Don would take a pill then forget which one he took and started to mix them up. Finally, he allowed me to take control of his medication. After the pills were separated, I prepared a matrix of what and when was to be taken during the day. The lady that rented from Don or I would put his medication out for him, and then hide the container.

Even though I had joined the Alzheimer's Association to understand the behaviors associated with the disease, it was still so confusing and tiring to be around Don. Some days we could have a conversation about the past which made me forget that he and I weren't really together anymore. I remember how I felt when he said he was filing for legal separation because he didn't want to be financially responsible for me. That really hurt. Yet, he still felt nothing changed in our relationship. I never understood that. He still wanted to be married, and live separately. I was a tax write off for him. I never understood his line of thinking. I lived my own life, but did help him when he was unable to function due to his illness.

When we talked about the past, I also forgot that he had dementia. We talked about our favorite cruises. Both of us liked the Grand Bahamas.

Laughing at the same time when we remembered the famous horse and buggy ride; the driver stopped the buggy, got off, went to the trunk of a car, reached in, and took out a paper bag, which we assumed was his lunch. In the meantime, the horse decided to walk backwards, so there we were rolling downhill towards an intersection where cars were weaving in and out. Thank goodness the driver saw what was happening, dropped his lunch, ran toward the horse, and grabbed it which stopped the horse before we were hit by a car that was just inches from us. When he jumped back onto the buggy he kept uttering *"Lo Siento, Lo Siento, I'm sorry Senor."* Those were the days when Don was healthy and vibrant. The following cruises were for Don to rest, because he got tired so easily.

During this time, Shawn was going to twelve-step meetings, working with his sponsor, doing all his assigned writing and care taking Don. Shawn loved Don. He was really the only male role Shawn had in his life. Don was like a father to him. Don loved Shawn and loved teaching him about anything that Shawn would listen to, from the history of Native people's weavings and pottery, to how to make a cup of coffee. For as nice as Don was to Shawn, he has been just as ornery with me. The criticism didn't stop, nor did the abusiveness. I would drive up in the morning and the lady that rented from him would tell me what his attitude was like. She was my "Don barometer."

Halloween night Don passed out candy dressed as his favorite character, Goofy, while my daughter, Shawn, and I took the kids out *Trick and Treating*. There were witches, cowboys, spacemen, action heroes and of course, lots and lots of princesses. We were walking with one of those princesses. I thought back to that night Don was so happy playing with all the kids, acting silly and goofy, like his favorite character, Goofy. The last time I saw Don enjoy Halloween that much was when I had a combination birthday and Halloween party at his home. His birthday is a couple days before Halloween, which was so fitting for him.

There was a casket in the foyer that held a dummy dressed in its best suit and would rise up when someone came in. Of course, we had a string attached to its arm and it was pulled up on someone's entry. His big house turned into the best spook house ever. Cobwebs with spiders, ghosts and eerie sounds. Food was prepared to look disgusting to include a chocolate cake that had worms in it. Of course, they were gummy worms. That was the last function his brother was able to attend, for he passed away shortly after. So, that party became an extra special day for Don.

Thanksgiving Don was not up for sharing that day with my family, however, we prepared a plate of food, which Shawn and I took to him. Thanksgiving was a holiday that did not really hold any special meaning for him. It was just another day. He said when he was growing up, his dad was never home for that holiday since he was in sales and was on the road, so their family really didn't celebrate the day. He carried that all through his life, which always caused friction between us. I loved Thanksgiving for it was a time for me to share my gratitude for and with my family.

In the midst of all that had been going on over the last several months, I was getting prepared for my Christmas project. Several of my friends and I would provide clothing for many families on the Navajo reservation. One of our Navajo lady friends would send us the names of families that needed more help than the tribe could give. The list included the names, ages, and sizes of each family member. So, there I was shopping with Shawn, picking out clothing for ten families, almost a hundred people in total. He was a big help to me even though he kept getting sidetracked with clothing for himself. I felt like I was shopping with my partner, for we had so much fun together and got along so well. What a crazy thought!

The shopping was completed now the wrapping began. When I lived with Don and did the wrapping at the house, he would complain and yell that there was paper and ribbon all over the dining room table. It was like he was jealous that I was doing something for someone other than him. He had never been supportive of this project, yet when he did go with me one year to help deliver the gifts he had fun with all the kids. He got to let out the silly side of himself, and the kids loved it.

There was one day that he really enjoyed himself. It was in the home of the Navajo girl that I had sponsored for many years. He passed out gifts to all the little kids and had them sit on his lap while he played Santa. He even had the grandmother sit on his lap while he sang to her. She also had fun along with all the kids watching. That was a nice experience for all of us.

As Shawn and I carried all the packages out of the store, I was exhausted, yet still felt full of energy. Why? I knew the answer, "I was happy." Over the last several months, Shawn and I had become so close. We talked about everything, shared our thoughts and emotions with each other, and laughed a lot. Yes, there were those times that we "butted heads," however, Shawn would be the one to say, "I think we need to talk about what just happened, or let's talk." Maybe if Don would have ever said anything like that or even took a speck of responsibility for any of our conflicts, we might still be together.

Well, all the gifts are wrapped; outfits for everyone and toys for every child. What a great feeling. The wrapping seemed not to take as long this time for Shawn helped where he could. Having a wrapping buddy was fun! I found myself wanting to always be with Shawn. It was so nice to hang out and share with someone without all the criticism that had been the main component of the relationship I had with Don. My feelings for Shawn were changing. I was seeing Shawn in a different way. I was seeing Shawn as a grown man, rather than the kid I was used to.

The van was packed and we were ready to go. Shawn was to stay with Don, however, none of my Christmas project buddies could go with me, so Shawn was elected to keep me company. I was excited to share this experience with him, and was actually glad that no one else was able to go.

The twelve-hour drive went by so quickly, starting off with a breakfast break at one of my fun favorite places to stop on the way. The restaurant had been the backdrop for a movie that came out many years ago, and pretty much looked the same today. It was the kind of restaurant that you would find on a deserted part of the old Route 66, which is exactly where it is. I loved sharing this new experience with Shawn for it became a new experience for me as well.

Entering the reservation was quite challenging for the rain and snow kept the driving visibility limited. The roads were slippery and dusk was turning to dark. Due to the reservation roads being so muddy, we were not able to make it to my friend's house and were instructed to meet her at a bazaar in a nearby town where she and other Navajo men and women were displaying and selling their homemade jewelry, weavings, pottery and baked goods. Whew, we made it.

It was late, I was exhausted from negotiating the roads, and we were lucky to have gotten a motel room, since so many people were stuck in the town because of the muddy roads. One room with two beds normally would not have been an uncomfortable situation for me. However, there was definitely a different kind of energy between Shawn and I. I have always been an authority figure in Shawn's life, however, it feels, and has been for quite a while now, more like a romantic partner, yet there has never been any romance between us. I have been picking up that same kind of energy from Shawn as well as innuendos alluding to a possible romantic or sexual interlude. Oh my, now we are sharing a room. I have been ignoring all of the suggestive comments and ignored my feelings and the situation once again, and went to sleep.

CHAPTER TWENTY-FIVE

BEST CHRISTMAS EVER

OUR TRIP BACK INCLUDED A STOP IN PHOENIX to see one of Joyce's friends. Actually, I knew her, too. It was fun having coffee with her. She is a nice lady and had come with Joyce to see me when I was in a board and care many years ago. We had all gone out for pizza and I always remembered her kindness. When we left her, we popped an audio book into the CD player and listened to it all the way home. That was cool, since I had never listened to an audio book before. It was a scary book and helped past the time on the drive. When I put that key in the door, my heart just sang…I am home, I am home, I am home!

Well, we spent the next couple of days sorting and wrapping presents for my sisters and brothers and their families. That was fun and felt so good. As I sat there eating chili cheese dogs with my sister and her family, I felt so much gratitude and joy. We had driven to see my family and brought gifts for everyone. This day was only in my dreams and now it was real. Here I was, just a year out of prison and 14 years separated from my family, enjoying something that I never thought possible. Joyce and I talked about the day as we drove back home.

Christmas Eve was the following night. There I was sitting in the back seat of Joyce's daughter's van on my way down to celebrate the evening with my new family. The celebration was at her in-laws and it was a wonderful evening. Lots of great food was set out buffet style. Turkey, beef, salads, potatoesand breads. A beautifully decorated Christmas tree stood in the corner with what looked like thousands of gifts piled haphazardly under it. The gifts were supposed to be for all the kids, however, there was one for me too. A box ended up in my hand that had a tag, which read "To Shawn from Santa." It was a beautiful blue shirt. There was also a tin of popcorn for Joyce and me as well. Sounds of ripping paper, laughing, and squeals filled the room from the kids that were getting their gifts from Santa. What a magical evening.

On the drive home, I kept hoping I could open my presents that had been sitting under our tree for the last couple of weeks. We walked through the door, I sat down by our tree, Joyce sat on the couch, and I dug into all my gifts. I ripped the paper off each package as fast as I could. Shoes, shirts, and jackets to match appeared. The jackets matched the shirts and the shirts matched the shoes. Pajamas, a robe, slippers, socks, shorts, complete outfits, both for day and night all lay on the floor around me. I was overwhelmed. None of it seemed real. There were still more packages under the tree. When Joyce told me they were for me, I was surprised, however, I dug in, once again.

A purple translucent face with a hand to it in a reflective position was in the first box I opened. I had seen this in a store several months before and wanted it, however, I chose a wall hanging with an inspirational quote instead. She knew I liked this sculpture and got it for me. I loved it, for it reminded me of me: pensive and reflective. Then I spotted a package that looked like music compact discs. Upon opening it, I saw a picture of my dad's singing group. There were several discs. My dad was part of three groups: The Vibrations, The Jayhawks and The Marathons. There was my entire dad's music. What a special gift! Having my dad's music was like putting a piece of my past together. He was a very talented man, and he passed that creativity on to his kids. There were other gifts. I was so overwhelmed. My dreams that night were not about sugarplums dancing in my head, they were about shoes, shirts, music, and a whole lot of feelings of gratitude.

As I reflected on the past several months, I felt so overwhelmed. Overwhelmed with feelings I hadn't felt for a long, long time. Here I was, living in a nice home, having my own space, having more clothing and toys than I ever had before, topped off with the reuniting of my family. In

Our Christmas tin of popcorn.

To Shawn from Santa.

a way, it was scary. If I thought about all the other times in my life when I was happy, I became fearful, for those times either I had to leave, or the situation changed in other ways. I pushed those feelings of fear away and decided just to bask in the joy of it all.

However, there was another issue at hand. Joyce and I had become very close. We were together all the time, going places, doing things together and of course, caring for Don together. I had always felt close to Joyce and loved her for the person she was. However, I was falling in love with her and really didn't know what to do with that. I started making innuendos. Some weren't appropriate, however, I wasn't sure what words to use to let her know in some way my feelings.

Holiday celebrations continued with Joyce's grandchildren opening their presents from Santa, dinner at her daughter's home, visiting my sisters and spending time with friends. What a way to spend my first Christmas with family and friends since I got my freedom from prison. In fact, I had not celebrated Christmas at all in years.

The most poignant time during the holidays was taking a five-year cake at an Alcoholics Anonymous meeting. I was five years clean and sober. My sponsor introduced me, presented me with a cake and Joyce and her family surrounded me and everyone sang happy birthday. Now, it was my turn to say something. I could not believe I was standing in front of over a hundred people sharing my story. It felt like I was in a fog, however, once I started talking, it was like my Higher Power just took over and words came out of my mouth that I didn't even know existed. I could feel the energy in the room and just basked in that energy. About a week later when Joyce and I were entering a local store, a woman yelled out, "Shawn," and walked toward me. I turned around but didn't recognize her. She said, "You saved my life last week." She could tell by my puzzled look that I had no idea what she was talking about. "I was at the meeting when you shared your story and it really touched me in a way that I was able to make the decision to turn my life around that day. Thank you for having the courage to share your story. It truly has made a difference in my life." I almost started to cry, to think that I, me, Shawn, actually made a difference in someone's life. She thanked me again and walked away. Those five minutes taught me that I needed to keep sharing my story. The profound significance of that moment still lingers in my heart.

CHAPTER TWENTY-SIX

COUNSEL

THE NEXT DAY I MANAGED TO GET us safely through the half broken, half sunken muddy main road to the roads that lead into the area that we were bringing gifts to. We managed to get to the Chapter house in the area, parked the car, and slid into the door, trying to figure out how to get all the gifts in without falling into the mud. With the help of Shawn and several Navajo men, all the packages made it safely to the tables inside.

It seemed that the roads have gotten worse and worse over the last twenty years. We used to be able to get through to all the different hogans and houses delivering the gifts personally to each child and elder. Those were fun days. Having a Santa with us made it very special. One year we had a caravan of 10 cars, vans, and trucks. Oh, so many elves! That year we provided for over 35 families. Over the years, people became less interested in coming in with me, mainly because of the cold, snowy weather and muddy impassable roads.

Shawn blew up basketballs, while I sorted the gifts into the different families. Over the next several hours, one by one, each family came and picked up their gifts. Some of them had to walk because their vehicles would not get through the mud.

As the day wound down, I suggested we get back to the town before dark since I knew whatever packages were left, my friend would see to it they made their way to the proper families. Got back to the motel, parked the car, and walked back over to the bazaar to see all what was available to buy. Oh, so much jewelry! A lot of weavings, as well! In the old days we would just sit around my friend's house. She would bring her jewelry out and some of her friends would bring theirs as well. That is how I used to shop. Everything changes. Nothing stays the same—sad in some ways.

I said my goodbye's, walked back to the motel and climbed into bed. I have to admit, thoughts of Shawn sleeping in the next bed kept me awake for some time. Leaving the next day was a good decision since we had perfect weather all the way home. No more mud!

Once home, we continued with our holiday celebrations first by visiting his family and what made that visit so special, besides the reuniting of a family, was that Shawn was able to get gifts for everyone. That was very important to him. Shawn was a most generous man. Here he was on disability, yet tried to give as much as he could and I was legally married to a multimillionaire who could never give of himself emotionally or financially. What a contrast in people.

Okay, so I had to deal with my feelings and really didn't know what to do. Of course, being somewhat of an authority figure in Shawn's life was a concern of mine. I know not to get involved with men who I counseled or were clients of mine, however, Shawn was never my client and I really didn't counsel him any more than what a friend would say. Then there was the age difference, which was really a concern of mine. So, I called the Interfaith Minister that I had been ordained with for counsel.

"So, here is the situation. I have fallen in love with Shawn. I'm not sure what to do with those feelings. I am also extremely attracted to him physically. If the situation was just that, it would not be as hard for me to deal with. He is interested in what I have to say, he shares his innermost thoughts and feelings with me. He is so encouraging of me and of others. He is loving and kind and although he is not formally educated, he is very intelligent." "What are your concerns?" Well, the age difference, for one. Also, I have been somewhat of an authority figure in his life." "So, you are concerned because you have helped him and have guided him at times?" "Yes, isn't that crossing some sort of line?" "It would be if you were seeing him in a formal counseling or therapeutic situation. However, he is not your client. He is someone you have always cared for and just tried to help." "Don't people in love help each other and guide each other as well?" "Of course," I replied. "So, the only issue I see is your idea that age makes a difference. Why should it?" "I don't know, maybe I am caught up in society's thinking on that."

After two hours of sharing my feelings, the situation, and listening to what she had to say, it seemed that there really was nothing wrong with acting on my feelings and addressing Shawn's. The only thing that had to change was that he no longer could call me "mom" if we were to move forward with our feelings. Of course I never had a problem with our different cultural backgrounds, nor our different socioeconomic differences, however, what it came down to for me was he age difference, and that really should not be an issue. I did feel much clearer and knew what I needed to do.

We went through the holidays together, sharing Christmas evening with my daughter's in laws and Christmas day with my daughter and her family. Christmas evening was a very special turning point for me. First, Don had been invited and declined, however, encouraged me to go with Shawn and to have fun. Then there was a gift for Shawn, which was so totally unexpected. When we got home that evening, I was so excited watching Shawn open all his presents that I had so much fun buying. The more I watched Shawn's enthusiasm, I could feel myself falling more in love with him. His appreciation and gratitude for life was so refreshing.

Don did come to celebrate Christmas dinner with us. He ate and like so many people after eating holiday dinners, fell asleep on the couch. He tried to enjoy the kids, but I could tell his energy was low. He didn't stay long since he wanted to get back home.

Shawn and I were back at his house the next day to help him with whatever he felt he needed to get done. "Know what I really want?" "What?" "I really want to go into my Jacuzzi bath; I'm so sore." "Okay, I think between Shawn and I we can do this." So there we were, together, lifting Don into the empty Jacuzzi tub. Once he was in I climbed back out to turn the water on. Don looked so small lying in the tub. He was enjoying his time soaking and letting the jets swirl around him. When he started to get wrinkly, I thought it best that his time be up in the tub before he shriveled up any further.

Getting Don out was much more of a problem than we thought. The hot water had completely relaxed his muscles, and Don was pretty much immobile. I drained the water from the tub, and climbed in. I could not lift Don enough for Shawn to grab him and lift him out of the tub. Don could not help at all, he was completely limp. Oh, I am not so sure this was such a good idea. To make things tougher, there was a step up to the tub, which had a very high raised side. Shawn climbed the step, knelt down so he could put his hands and arms under Don's. After much struggling, we got Don into a position where Shawn could carry him to his bed. He was so weak, that we dressed him in his tee shirt and shorts and tucked him in for the night. What an ordeal. There were no more Jacuzzi baths. Boy, what if I had done that on my own. We would still be in that tub.

When we got home, I sat up for a while thinking. Thinking about Don, how I met him, our on and off relationship for 12 years, my nine year marriage to him, living with my daughter and her husband after Don broke his neck, helping him through that as well as helping him and ultimately taking care of him due to his diagnosed chronic nerve condition.

During this time my mom had a stroke which left her with hydrocephalus or more commonly known as "water on the brain." So over the next five or six years she started to have trouble walking and went from a cane to not being able to walk at all. My sister became her caretaker since they lived together in Chicago and I took over her finances. I was going back and forth from California to Chicago every two or three months to see how she was doing and the last couple of visits it became clear to me that my mom needed to live in a nursing home where she could get the proper care she needed. She was having hallucinations and was becoming delusional. After a year in the nursing home, she started to come back to life and her mind cleared. I didn't think mom would live more than a year after she moved in, however, it has been over five years that she has been there and although she cannot walk she is doing great. I had quit my counseling at the alcohol and drug rehabilitation centers to start my own private counseling and coaching practice and wrote a self-help book during this time as well. And now, I was falling in love with Shawn and it felt really good, but really scary as well. What a crazy decade this has been.

New Year's was approaching and I knew what I needed to do. I needed to address this with Shawn.

CHAPTER TWENTY-SEVEN

BRINGING IN THE NEW YEAR

A s WE CAME UPON NEW YEAR'S, Joyce and I were closer than ever. I was sitting on the patio just hanging out thinking about going to her daughter's that evening. Joyce came out, sat down, and started a conversation with me about how she noticed my interest in her. She said she also had an attraction to me. I could tell she was nervous talking to me about what was going on between us. I wasn't nervous, but surprised that she was able to bring it up. Although, I knew something had to happen because the attraction was just getting stronger between us.

We discussed what to do about the sexual tension between us. She said if sex was introduced into our relationship, it would change, and what would happen afterwards would be an unknown. She was also concerned that it could become confusing or emotionally damaging to me somehow because I was newly sober five years and she had been an authority figure in my life and I even called her mom from time to time. Then there was the age difference that concerned her.

I felt that if we added sex to our relationship, it would become deeper. Since I believed that the sexual tension between us was there, however, I felt that we had something deeper. I knew it would not mess me emotionally. I had a mental illness, but I wasn't stupid. The newly sober thing was something that the 12-step meetings preached. When I attended the meetings, I would often hear not becoming involved in a relationship the first year of sobriety, however, I was five years sober. The age did not make a difference to me, in fact, that was a turn on to me.

The conversation ended for the time being and we decided if it were to happen, we would let it happen naturally. We both got ready to go to her daughter's to celebrate New Year's Eve. Although I had fun with the kids, all I could think about was the conversation that Joyce and I had, wondering if and when we would pursue our feelings for each other. I didn't have to wonder long, for when we got home, we began to hug, different than our usual quick hug hello or goodbye. This was different, so I took a chance and kissed Joyce, and she responded. I will always remember that moment. It is true; time does stand still in a moment like that.

We took care of our sexual tension at midnight. Fireworks were going off outside. However, they could have been going off in my head for this is one celebration I will never forget. Bringing in the New Year by consummating our relationship is what New Year's Eve is all about!

I had fallen in love with Joyce before that evening, however, our night together just brought those feelings deeper into my heart and soul. I so wanted this relationship and yet I was unsure of Joyce's feelings toward me.

As we got closer, our relationship morphed into a deep romantic one. Joyce, in spite of her fear, let herself fall in love with me.

We were still taking care of her husband, even though their marriage had been over for years. I loved Joyce for so many reasons. One of them is she stepped up to take care of her husband, even though they were not together anymore. When they were together, he was mean to her and critical of her. He would not get a divorce because he didn't want to pay for it. So, she was at an impasse.

When Don's neighbor called her to let her know that he had needed help, she immediately went back up to his home and started to take care of him. She drove him shopping, to the doctors, to art auctions—anywhere he wanted to go. There were times she had to dress him and clean him up. Don yelled, criticized, or argued the entire time she helped him. The chronic neurological disorder coupled with an injured spinal cord from his broken neck injury caused him trouble walking. Therefore, I had to lift or carry him at times.

As the months went on, I thought Joyce was going to have a nervous

breakdown. She tried her hardest to make him happy and to accommodate his needs, however, no matter what she did or how hard she tried, it
was never right or good enough.

Joyce took his keys away so he could not drive and he argued with her
every day about getting his keys back. One night he wanted to go somewhere, and he demanded that she take him right that minute. She suggested that they wait until the next day because of heavy traffic. However,
he insisted that she take him and started a temper tantrum. Joyce said okay
and they went to the car.

As she was driving he was criticizing the way she was driving, and
went on and on about other things in her life. She turned the car around
and came back to the house. She got out and went around to the passen-
ger side of the car to help him out. He refused to get out of the car. He
folded his arms and just sat there, defying her just like a cranky child. She
asked him nicely, then more firmly and finally she just broke down and
cried. He just would not get out of the car. He opened her glove com-
partment and threw out whatever he found. Insurance cards, manuals, as
well as maps, hit the ground.

Then, all of a sudden, he reached up his hand and asked for help to get
out and instead of pulling himself out of the car, he pulled her in. Joyce
struggled not to lose her footing and fall in. She backed out and once
again asked him to get out of the car. He finally did and took with him
anything he could find in the car. As he was walking to the front door,
she asked him for the papers he took from the car. He threw them on the
ground and when she bent down to get them, he tried to hit her with
his cane.

He went into his house and locked the door. He took her keys and
wouldn't give them back. I finally convinced him to do so. That was quite
an evening. The behavior he displayed was mostly due to the dementia,
but his personality was also like that, only not as intense.

We got by that incident and the next day they talked. He felt like he
was out of control of his own life. He was right; he was. He felt that everyone but him was controlling his life—doctors, caretakers and Joyce. He
said he wanted to drive and that Joyce had no right to keep his keys. He
had called an auto club and they were coming to make new keys for him.
Ultimately, he got his keys back, and agreed only to drive to his bank and

the store, which were literally six blocks away. So that is how it went for a couple of weeks until that fateful night.

CHAPTER TWENTY-EIGHT

A HAVEN IN THE STORM

NEW YEAR'S EVE WAS MY BEST NIGHT EVER. It was a haven in a storm. I felt so loved and cared for. Yes, we had sex, but the feelings and energy around us were so intense, so much love. I was very nervous when we got home from my daughter's for I knew that tonight would be the night. When Shawn hugged me and kissed me, I no longer felt nervous, I felt safe and secure. He was so caring, so loving, so sure of himself. Although, I found out later he was just as nervous as I was, maybe even more.

I no longer denied my feelings. I was in love with Shawn. What was next? Was he in love with me? I knew he loved me, but was it romantic love. Time would tell. I wasn't sorry that we acted on our attraction to each other since it had been a long time since I had been with anyone in a very loving way. Don hadn't been loving for so long and sex had not been part of our lives for over six years, a combination of me not being turned on by his criticism and ultimately his inability due to his illness. Shawn was a haven in a storm, a storm that was hurling me around emotionally.

Our attraction to each other had gone unnoticed by most of my friends, so I thought. One morning I was having breakfast with a friend and all of a sudden she said, "Do you know that you are in love with Shawn?" My mouth dropped open and before I could answer, she added, "I could see the way you looked at each other one night when we all got together for dinner." I didn't deny it and shared with her what had been going on. She was so supportive and saw absolutely no problem with it. I was so grateful for her love, kindness, and support, because the days with Don had been so physically and emotionally trying. I was just about spent.

All the while taking care of Don, Shawn and I were very careful to not let on to our friends about the relationship change. I believe Don knew. When I thought back to last year, he said in one of our conversations that he just assumed that Shawn and I were having sex. That really caught me by surprise since Shawn and I did not have that kind of relationship then. I don't think Don cared one way or the other if Shawn and I were involved, sexually or romantically. He knew he had not been emotionally present for me for many years. I'm not sure if Don really knew how to love, or just plain didn't want to. He used to say, "I only criticize people I care about." I guess that is how he loved, by being critical.

As the next several weeks went by, Don became more and more belligerent with some moments of clarity in which we could talk. What an emotional roller coaster.

One day returning Don back to his home after taking him to run his errands, he turned to Shawn and said, "Be good to Joyce; always take care of her." I thought what an odd thing to say. Later that night, I received a phone call from Don and when I answered he said, "Hi, it is me. I just wanted to tell you that you have always been a very good wife." Wow, where was that coming from? A couple minutes later, I received another phone call from the lady who rented from Don, for she had heard the phone call through the monitors in her place. She was amazed to hear what Don said, and really couldn't believe it. He was actually nice. We both thought it was a strange phone call

On my way home the next day from spending time with a friend, Don called and asked me if I would take him to an auction the next day and I told him I would. He said he was going to drive down to the store and I asked him not to go, that I would come up and get him, however, he said, "I'm only going down the block." Again, I asked him not to go, but he insisted he was going. "I promise I will only go to the store down the block." He never kept that promise.

The phone rang, I looked at the clock, and it was a little after midnight.

I knew there was something wrong.

"Hello."

"Joyce, the police are here looking for Don's wife" said Don's renter.

"Why, is Don in trouble?"

"They want to talk with you."

Another women's voice asked, "Is this Mrs. Bennett?"

"Yes, this is Joyce."

"We would like to talk to you about your husband."

"Do you want me to come to the house?"

"No, we will come to where you live."

"Is Don okay?"

"We can talk when we get there."

#
A DARK NIGHT

I HEARD THE PHONE RING, but I thought it was part of my dream until I heard Joyce say, "Hello." Being only half awake, I couldn't really hear what Joyce was saying and fell back asleep. Something woke me back up and I realized that Joyce was up and all the lights were on. I looked at the clock, saw that it was past midnight, and immediately knew the phone call that she received was some sort of emergency.

Shaking off the fog of sleep, which proved to be very difficult due to the medication I had taken before going to bed, got up, put some clothes on and found Joyce downstairs. She shared the conversation she had with the police and I knew, just knew it was bad news. I had a sinking feeling in the pit of my stomach. Joyce walked outside and I'm not sure what I did. I was feeling very anxious, so I probably went on the patio and had a cigarette.

When the police car pulled up, Joyce looked like she expected to see Don in the back seat, arrested for some violation, however, when she did not see him, her facial expression changed along with her body language. She really looked scared.

I felt scared. We all sat down.

CHAPTER THIRTY

A FEAR REALIZED

STANDING OUTSIDE WAITING FOR THE POLICE CAR to pull up seemed like an eternity. Finally, I spotted headlights pulling into our complex and watched as the car got closer and closer. As the squad car pulled up I expected to see Don in the back seat of the car. I figured he must have gotten into some sort of trouble which got the police involved.

When the squad car came to a stop I did not see anyone in the back seat. In fact, the only one I saw was a policewoman getting out from the driver's side of the car. She walked around the car and as she approached me she said, "Let's go inside." I turned and led the way into the condo.

She told me her name and asked me to sit down. I did, and she took a seat next to me.

"Do you know where your husband was tonight?"

"Yes, he said he was going to the store down the street."

"I am sorry to have to tell you that your husband was in a single-car accident and passed away tonight."

Even though I heard her words, it was like she was speaking to me in a tunnel. She repeated herself, "Ma'am, your husband passed away tonight; he was in a car accident. It was a single-car accident. No one else was hurt."

I knew there was something wrong when I couldn't reach Don in the evening, a time that he should have been home from the store, since the store was only a couple of blocks from his house. Shawn had gotten up shortly after the phone call and was wondering what was going on. I had told him what the police had said and he immediately became anxious. When I finally was able to come back to what the officer was saying I saw Shawn, who was now sitting across from us, hit the floor with his fist and heard him say, "Damn." He then got up, left, went out onto the patio, and lit a cigarette.

Even though this was our biggest fear, I never really believed it would happen. A car accident took his life. I thought back to what he had said to Shawn yesterday and to my phone call from him just last night. Somehow, he knew he would be leaving this plane soon.

The lady that was renting the little apartment above Don's garage had also come with the police. She had a sense of what had happened and came along to support us. I was so grateful that she was here. She could see that Shawn was very distraught and went out to the patio to try to calm him a bit. I could hear her say, "I am so sorry Shawn. I know you were very close to him." "Yes, he was always there for me." "Well, from what the officer said, he didn't suffer." Shawn seemed to get a grip on his emotions, for I heard the screen door open and watched as both of them came back into the living room.

"Mrs. Bennett?" "Yes." "As I said before, your husband did not suffer, he was killed instantly. There was an S curve and he did not turn, he continued to go straight. He hit the curb, the car flipped over and his neck broke." "I was afraid something like this would happen if he drove. That is why I drove him anywhere he wanted or needed to go." The officer asked me if I was okay and when I assured her I was, she said, "I am so sorry," and left.

How many movies have we all seen where the police roll up and knock on someone's door to deliver the bad news that a family member had died? Oh, so many! Yet, to be the one to experience that dreaded visit; the words that are spoken is surreal. You hear the words and see their mouth move, but neither registers in your brain. I understood why so many people in the movies scream, "No, it's not true." Those were my first thoughts, only my words did not come out very eloquently for I heard myself say, "Are you sure?" Now that I think back that was a ridiculous of a statement. It is amazing how the mind and body deals with or not deals with SHOCK.

I felt like I had to get out of the house and go where the accident happened. Not sure why, however, I just had to go. Shawn and I got in the car and with Don's renter following, drove up and down the streets close to where the officer said it happened. I never found it and proceeded to drive to Don's house calling my son-in-law on the way. He is a funeral director and I knew that he would know what to do next.

Entering Don's house we all agreed that the silence was deafening. No dog, no Don and although Don's dog had recently died, because he always had a dog, it just seemed natural for a dog to greet us. Rufus was an 85-pound dog that Don and I had gotten off the Navajo reservation. He was 55 pounds at the time, and filthy from eating out of the garbage bins outside the little boarding school where we found him.

It was amazing how Rufus could open a can of food with his teeth to get to what was inside. After a while, he stopped stealing cans out of the cabinets and off the counters. He finally realized there was always food in his dish. Don named him Rufus, since he was kind of a clumsy dog, although it was more like he hadn't grown into his skin yet since he was only a year old. After having him checked out by the vet we found out that he had a bullet in him and a BB in his head. Obviously, he was used as target practice. Rufus lived a little more than five years before he developed an illness that took his life. That was during the time that Don had trouble walking and although he wanted another dog, he knew that may not be the best thing for either of them. As it was, the lady that rented from Don had walked Rufus for him since he was not able to do so after a while. Memories of Rufus flooded my mind as I continued walking into the house.

CHAPTER THIRTY-ONE

SAYING GOODBYE

THAT WAS A VERY DARK NIGHT FOR ME. I loved Don very much. He was the only real male role model I had in my life. The money he sent me when I was in prison, enabled me to buy food from the prison canteen. The collect calls I would make to Don kept me going for he always had something funny and inspiring to say to me.

The next few weeks, after that dark night, Joyce, her sister-in-law, and I went through Don's personal belongings and packed up things for his daughter. Some things were donated and given away. It was all so overwhelming.

Apparently, Don had driven farther into town than just the corner store. Joyce tracked his movements through his credit card statement. "Look at this. He went and got tacos way on the other side of town. What was he doing so far away?" "That's crazy, since there is a taco place not far from his house." "Yes, that is the one that you and he used to go to. Well, I can only assume that when he was coming back toward the house and more than likely he got disoriented and lost and got off the wrong exit since the accident was on a street that he never drove on."

The day after the accident we went to where the accident happened. We saw where the street became an S turn and where his car hit the curb. Because of the apparent speed he was going when he hit the curb on the other side of the road, the car flipped onto its roof, sheared off a fire hydrant and a utility pole, and then the car flipped back onto its tires.

There were city workers repairing the utility pole when we rolled by and when we parked and walked around where the van up-righted itself, we found several of Don's personal items. No wonder he was killed instantly.

Don didn't want a memorial service, so we had a small gathering at a neighbor's house. We all shared a little story or memory about Don. There were two poster pictures of Don that made him seem as if he were looking at all of us. Maybe he was; who knows? Don had requested cremation and his ashes sent to the VA cemetery in Santa Fe, New Mexico. So that is what Joyce did.

Before he was cremated, Joyce and I went to say our goodbyes to Don in a private room at the cemetery. I wasn't going to go in, however, after Joyce came out, I decided to go in to say goodbye. I walked over to the table that Don was laying on and I immediately felt a sense of calm, for he looked like he was sleeping. "Don, I am so sorry. I am so, so sorry. Thank you for all the help you gave me. Thank you keeping my attitude up when I was in prison. Thank you for all the money you sent to me. I love you. You were a good friend to me. Thank you. I love you."

Joyce started planning a trip to see her mom in Chicago. It had been many months since we had been there due to taking care of Don. Since his daughter was handling the estate, there wasn't much for us to do, so we decided to drive across the county, which would allow us to decompress a bit. The last year had been so very difficult and stressful. I could tell they had taken their toll on Joyce. It was the beginning of "our" journey together.

CHAPTER THIRTY-TWO

A GOODBYE GATHERING

DON PROPOSED TO ME WEARING A MEXICAN SOMBRERO and getting down on one knee in the lobby of the dental office where I worked. He loved doing fun, silly things to make me laugh. That was the beginning of my marriage to Don. After a twelve-year-long relationship, we decided to get married and there was never a dull moment." There I was, standing in front of thirty-something people all waiting to pay their respects and get some closure on their relationship with Don. I was hoping that I was coming across a bit sad, however, in reality, I was relieved. The emotional abuse, coupled with his physical illness and dementia had just about done me in.

"I met Don when I took my daughter to preschool since he was the only dad there and looked a little lost. We connected and from that time on Don and I were fast friends. Our daughters played together and my husband and I had a lot of fun with Don. He was a good man and a fun friend."

"Don got me into the business of dealing art. I was struggling to make ends meet for my son and I when I met Don at a Native American antique show. We talked and he educated me in Native American baskets and told me to learn as much as I could on my own and get into the business of being an Indian Trader. Dealers in Native American Indian antique art are called Indian Traders, so, eventually, I became one. When Don invited me to do his show, I was so excited and did very well. That was oh, so long ago and oh, so many memories ago. I will miss Don's smiling face at the shows."

Person after person shared stories about Don until just about everyone had said something. At the end, we all held hands and said a prayer. It was done. A celebration of a man's life boiled down to some stories, a prayer, and sandwiches. I gave a sigh of relief and went home.

Don's daughter was handling the estate so there was not much for me to do after we went through and sorted Don's things. So, I decided to drive to Chicago to visit my mom and sister since I hadn't seen them for a while. Shawn was up for the trip.

I let go of the past and decided to move forward and embrace a new future. I was so ready.

CHAPTER THIRTY-THREE

A NEW BEGINNING

W E STARTED "OUR JOURNEY" LATE ONE AFTERNOON. I was so excited. We had some things to take care of in the morning and there was also a delay on some necessary medication. So, by the time we headed out of town, it was the middle of the afternoon. We stopped in Newbury Springs, just east of Barstow, at the Bagdad Café. We had watched the movie, *Bagdad Café*, sometime the previous year. So we stopped there for a bite to eat.

The movie did not really catch on in the United States. However, it was a big hit in Europe. A German lady and her husband were on their way to Las Vegas, when their car either slid off the road or got stuck. Either way, the lady decided to leave him and go it on her own. As the husband got the car back on the road, he stopped, threw out her coffee pot, and what he thought was her suitcase. In reality it was his suitcase. So, pulling her, really his, suitcase she started walking down a narrow desolate road in the desert and came upon a little motel and a failing diner called Bagdad Café. She stays at the little motel and befriends the woman owner of the diner. Ultimately, wearing her husband's clothes she brings in a booming business at the café by performing magic.

It was not really a typical drama. It became a cult film in Europe and a lot of tourists come from all over Europe to see the Bagdad Café. In fact, as we were sitting having coffee, a tour bus pulled up with tourists from France. So, if we hadn't started out late, we would have missed all the excitement at the Bagdad Café.

We got back on the highway, drove for several hours, found a motel somewhere in Arizona and spent the night. "Our journey, our journey, we began our journey" kept running through my head as I lay in bed. The next thing I remember the light was steaming into our room from underneath the blinds. We were up early the next morning, ate breakfast, and then headed for the Grand Canyon in Arizona.

As we drove through the Grand Canyon National Park on our way to the rim of the canyon, the excitement rose within me. My life was so different now. It was as if I was living someone else's life. While these thoughts were running through my head, we parked the car. I came back to reality, got out, grabbed our dog, and started down the path that led to the rim.

This is amazing! Amazing is the only word that came to my mind as I looked at the view in front of me. It was like looking at an artist's pallet. I had never seen anything like this and I was taking everything in.

I told Joyce, "I wish I was a bird so I could fly, for I would fly everywhere over and in this canyon."

"Yes, it is amazing. The first time I saw this, I was overwhelmed. Looking into the canyon gives me a sense of how small I really am. You can go down into the canyon on a donkey, although I have never done that. I think it would be a little scary."

"No way you gonna get me to ride a donkey into the canyon."

We laughed and walked along the rim. Each step I took the colors and view changed. The depth and colors of the canyon were breathtaking.

"Would you like some coffee?" Joyce asked.

"Yes, thank you."

I sat with our dog, Pablo, and just looked out into the canyon, as Joyce went to get us coffee. As we sat there drinking our coffee and just enjoying our time together in this beautiful setting, many people came up to us and started talking. We were like people magnets. I believe we just gave off an energy of love and happiness and people wanted to be around us. Of course, Pablo had something to do with it also, for people thought he was so cute.

"Well, should we continue our journey?" Joyce asked. I nodded, and loved hearing the words "our journey." Reluctantly we left to continue "our journey". Driving through Arizona, and into New Mexico, we arrived in Santa Fe in the late evening. The little casitas, as it is called, that we stayed in was perfect. What a perfect ending to a perfect day.

We spent the next couple of days enjoying our time together. Our favorite spot to spend time together was a wonderful teahouse that was nestled amongst trees. Sitting and talking with Joyce in this serene place was magical. Gosh, I was so in love with her and at times couldn't believe I was with her.

Strolling hand in hand through the downtown plaza park was so romantic. Shopping under the roof of one of the buildings was so fun.

"I want to buy you some earrings."

"Oh, you don't have to."

"I want to. I want to buy you a lot of things. How about these?"

"Yes, those are really nice. They are what you call the man in the maze design. I like them."

"I'll take these and also these."

"Shawn, two pair?"

"Yes, I like both of them."

"Thank you, I love both pairs."

It felt really good to be able to buy Joyce those earrings. I learned later that Native Americans sell their jewelry, pottery, weavings or any other items that they have made is a Santa Fe custom. I was living life large!

Filled with mixed emotions we left Santa Fe. My experience there was so wonderful that I just wanted to stay and have more of the same. However, we were on our way to Chicago and needed to continue "our journey."

My Santa Fe look.

Taking a break in Texas.

CHAPTER THIRTY-FOUR

SANTA FE

H ERE I AM DRIVING ACROSS THE DESERT with Shawn and it doesn't seem real. How many times have I driven this route? Too many to count! In the past I either was driving with Don to help with the shows, or driving to Santa Fe to meet him. Not to mention the over 25 years of driving to the reservation. This time I am driving with someone who is my future. Someone who makes me feel good about me. Someone who loves and adores me. Someone who actually listens to what I say and doesn't criticize me or put me down. But the best part is that I am driving with someone who I love and adore and that is the best part.

"Shawn, how are you doing?" I asked.

"Good."

"Does this seem real to you, us being together?"

"Yes, it had to happen. We were meant to be together. I love it and love you."

"Thanks, I think so too."

"I can't wait for you to be my wife."

"Really? What about the age difference."

"That doesn't matter to me. It's what's in your heart that matters to me."

"That is so sweet."

As I continue driving, I started going over all what had taken place this past couple of years. Doctors, doctors, and more doctors. When we weren't at doctor's visits I was helping Don with shows. The last time I helped Don in Santa Fe I was carrying a ladder in one hand and a piece of art in the other from the car into the convention center when a wasp flew up my sleeve and sat on my upper arm and there was nothing I could do. My sleeves were short, so it did not have too far to fly up to land and sit on the bottom of my upper arm. It stung me, but unlike what I remember a bee sting being, it seemed to sting me more than once and it hurt like hell. Finally, I was able to put the ladder down and the piece of art and swiped at the wasp and it did fly off my arm.

One of the dealers came over and helped me by getting one of the security personnel to get me an antihistamine. Everyone was concerned about me. Don came in from the car. We told him what happened, and his comment was, "Whatever." Typical, typical, typical. My being stung was of no interest or concern to him. Stuff like that happened all the time. Now, I am sitting next to someone who cares what goes on with me, or to me, and wants to help and protect me from any harm. He makes me feel loved. I haven't felt that for many, many years.

As the highway unfolded before us, the New Mexican and Texas landscapes were fleeting full of different colors, animals, and terrain. When we arrived at the border of New Mexico and Texas we spotted a sign that read "Private truck stop." Stopping to see what a "private truck stop" looked like, and to our surprise, it held many treasures. An antique car display was one of them.

"Look at all these old cars, wow!" "Yes, I actually had one of those over there, the white one, although mine was in blue and it was a convertible." We walked through the display of cars that represented different makes, models, and years. "I've never seen cars like these." "Shawn, most of these cars are older than you." Shawn was getting a quick education in antique cars and I was reminiscing about the blue convertible I had many years ago.

An old soda machine, antique tools, an old jukebox, radios, and even some antique cooking utensils were part of the display as well. "See that old jukebox." "Yes." "Well, we had one in our basement. It held the old size 78 records, the size my mom and dad listened to. I used to roller skate in the basement and practiced some of what I thought were fancy moves with the music." "Cool." We made a little donation to the makeshift museum and walked toward the gift shop.

Taking a break in Texas.

The gift shop was loaded with wonderful goodies as well. We shopped for treasures laughed at all the fun signs for cowboys like "Don't squat on your spurs", looked at jewelry, and lotions and of course Shawn bought some lotion and bought me a necklace and earring set that is still one of my favorites today. "Well, we sure had fun." "Yes, we did, but then we always do, don't we?" "Yes, we do!" Shawn walked out and I heard him say, "Don't squat on your spurs." And then he broke out in a thunderous laugh. When I thought about it, that was a pretty funny sign. I started to laugh too!

CHAPTER THIRTY-FIVE

MEDIUM RARE

D ON'T SQUAT ON YOUR SPURS. Oh boy, that was funny. That sure was fun. I've never been anywhere like we had just been." "Yes, that was fun and I sure like the jewelry you got me. You sure have good taste and a big heart as well. Thanks again, I love them."

Happy and content, I watched as the scenery changed from the southwest desert and far off mountains to the flat terrain of Oklahoma. We stopped in Elk City, Oklahoma, saw no elk, only a couple of motels and a few restaurants.

Joyce had been talking about having a steak for the longest time and had me looking forward to one as well. We pulled into the first of the three motels we saw. They didn't take dogs; the second one didn't either. The third motel was tucked away in the back of what looked like a truck lot and looked a bit shabby, but they took dogs. So after checking into the motel that would take our dog, we were about to make our way to the steak restaurant that the manager of the motel suggested. Actually it was the only one in town. Joyce said, "Do you smell that?" "Yes, I do." The room the motel had available was a smoking room. The smell was overwhelming to Joyce, and even though I smoke, I had to admit the odor was strong.

Joyce sped down to the office and came back with incense. When she checked us in, she noticed that there were Buddhas in the lobby and the manager appeared to be from India. Therefore, she concluded he may have incense and she was right. "Let's light the incense before we go so when we get back the room will smell a little better." "Good idea"

The Wagon Wheel was the kind of restaurant where you place your food order, carry your tray with drinks and the server brings you your dinner. After standing by the counter for several minutes, reading the menu, which was a blackboard on the wall, we ordered a half-pound rib eye that we decided to split. "How do you want that cooked?" We both said at the same time—"medium rare."

"Boy, I can't wait to eat. I am starving." "Me too." As I looked around at all the cowboy stuff on the walls I started thinking of that sign, "Don't squat on your spurs." This would be the place to see that sign. My thoughts were interrupted by a man delivering our meal. Joyce divided the steak, looked at it, and asked "Is this too rare for you?" Looking back on the situation, I should have answered that it was too rare, since it was not only bright red, but really hard to chew. However, I knew that Joyce liked it rare, so I said "Nah, it is fine." I found out a little later that she was hoping that I didn't like it so she could send it back. We each wanted to please the other, however, by doing that, neither one of us ate our dinner and got into an argument over the situation. We decided from that point on that we would always keep it real with each other, always speaking our truth. We were learning about each other on "our journey." I think our dinner that night was cheese and crackers. The only one that was satisfied was Pablo.

CHAPTER THIRTY-SIX

SORRY FOR THE INCONVENIENCE

S WE ENTERED THE FREEWAY SYSTEM heading into St. Louis I really appreciated the technology that could help me negotiate the system. So confusing, there roads everywhere and I didn't know where I was going. I had a flashback to the last time I went through St. Louis which was when I left Chicago on my way to a new life in California many years ago.

My ex-husband wanted to take the drive out West with us. So, he and I, along with our children and niece made the three-day drive. One of our stopovers was Albuquerque, New Mexico for the night. We had just checked into a nice hotel, put our bags in the room and were on our way to the restaurant, looking forward to having an enjoyable dinner, when our son somehow hit his head on the wall. Blood was dripping down his head as well as the wall. I thought he must have hit that wall pretty hard. We got towels for both. Holding a towel on my son's head, we set out to find our way to a hospital. We found one that was a hospital for the Native Americans from the nearby reservations. The hospital took us anyway when we explained our situation.

We were escorted to a cot in the emergency room.

"Well, son, what happened here? You have quite a cut."

"My cousin and I were goofing around, she pushed me, and I pushed her back, tripped, and hit the wall." So, now I knew what really happened.

When asked how it happened, neither one could really tell me. Kids!

"Well, I'm going to numb the area of your head so when I stitch the cut you won't feel it."

I sat holding my son's hand as, what looked like a gigantic needle made its way to his head. "Did that hurt honey?"

"No."

"Wow, I thought, it sure looked like it would have hurt."

After five or so stitches, we left and made our way back to the hotel. Instead of the nice dinner we had planned, we all ended up with fast food for dinner.

As I continued to think about that trip, we found a motel right off the freeway near the airport. It was across from a waffle restaurant. Shawn and I decided to stop for the night. Again, I flashed back to that trip and memories of my ex-husband and me pulling up in front of a motel in Hollywood across from a pancake house. We were so glad to finally have made it to California and Hollywood at that. The hotel had an opening so we checked in and settled in for the night. That night we were awakened by loud footsteps, yelling and slamming of doors, when all of a sudden our door was pushed open and a light was flashed in our eyes. I heard my ex-husband say, "What's going on?" "Just checking rooms, sir, sorry for the inconvenience." We got up and went into the hall just in time to see several girls being marched out by the police. What a scary night.

That morning sitting in the pancake house we found out from some of the locals that there had been a raid at the motel where we had stayed. The raid ended in a prostitution bust. A prostitution ring had been operating out of this motel and apparently it was some sort of sting operation. Somehow we were lucky enough to be part of all that excitement. Yeah, right! That was the beginning of my new life!

I shared that story with Shawn as we walked to the waffle restaurant for dinner. When we crashed out for the night I had thoughts that the door would be pushed open and a light would be flashed in my eyes. Those thoughts didn't last all that long for the next thing I remember it was morning. The night had come and gone without incident.

CHAPTER THIRTY-SEVEN

THE NURSING HOME

OUR RIDE THE NEXT DAY WAS ESPECIALLY NICE. I think it was partly due to my excitement in finally reaching our destination, which we did in the early afternoon.

With Italian beef sandwiches in our hands, we walked into the nursing home early evening and surprised Joyce's mom. She was so happy to see us and even happier to see the sandwiches. We ate, talked, and laughed until it was time for her mom to go to bed. She was so happy and I was happy because she was.

The next morning, Joyce's mom was again, so excited to see us. We talked and laughed some more. We told her about us being romantically involved and that we were going to get married. She seemed genuinely happy for us. We were the hit of the nursing home. We were the odd couple.

We stayed at Joyce's sister's apartment and Pablo stayed with Joyce's cousin, Elaine. Pablo was a very happy dog, since he got to stay and play all day. The nursing home is where we spent our days.

"So tell me—when did you guys fall in love?" Joyce's mom asked.

"New Year's Eve."

"Did you talk about getting together or did it just happen?"

"Both."

I enjoyed listening to Joyce and her mom talk, reminiscing about their past.

"Mom, do you remember when you gave all my blouses away to one of those donation centers?"

"Oh yes, but how did that happen?"

"I had put all my blouses in the bathtub before I left for school and was planning on washing them when I got home. However, when I got home none of my blouses were there."

Laughing, Joyce's mom said, "I remember now. I gave them away to someone who came to the door looking for donations. That was crazy. I just wanted to give him something. I felt sorry for him, so when I saw the blouses in the tub, I just didn't think. I grabbed them and gave them to the guy at the door. I am so sorry."

Joyce laughed and they continued to share stories. I got antsy, and went outside where I could have a cigarette and talk to the aides who were on their break.

"Who are you here to visit?"

"My fiancé's mother."

"What's her name?"

"Dorothy."

"Her daughter is your fiancée?"

"Yes, she is sixty-nine years old and I love that she is older that me."

"Wow, she doesn't look sixty-nine; she looks like she is in her forties. Can I ask how old you are?"

"Yes, I am thirty-one."

"You both are blessed to have found each other, for it is obvious you guys are in love."

Meeting new people always makes me happy. I learn new things from talking with people and I am able to share new things with them. I like making people laugh and feel good when they enjoy my stories. I don't always have filters when I talk with other people, so they learn more about me than I intended. Sometimes I say things that may not be so appropriate for the situation, however, I am learning.

"Mom, do you remember when you and your girlfriend got locked in a car dealership?"

"I sort of remember that. How did that happen?"

Mom in a kazoo band.

Mom singing solo for the first time.

Papier-mâché dolls mom made.

"You and dad were looking at cars with your girlfriend and her husband. The dealership was about to close so the men decided to leave and go home and you and your girlfriend were going out somewhere, so you didn't leave with them. Before you left the dealership you and your girlfriend went into the restroom. Apparently you both were in there a long time, for when you came out, the dealership was closed. So, there you were in a closed business with no way out. Those were the days of no cell phones and you couldn't get a hold of dad right away, so you used one of the phones there and called the police."

"Yes, now I remember. I was so embarrassed. Once we got out of there, we left as fast as we could. We didn't want to wait around for the owner to show up since the police jimmied the door and the lock broke. They should have checked the restroom before they locked up."

"You're right. Today, not only do businesses have alarms, you would never have been able to leave right after the police got you out."

"We sure got ourselves in some goofy situations."

"You sure did."

When I returned, I said, "I met some of the nurse's aides outside and they all knew your mom. I told them that we were getting married and I told them our ages."

"Shawn, why did you tell them?"

"Because you don't look your age, number one, and number two, I like that you are older. I am proud of that. No one could believe you're sixty nine. They said you looked like you were in your forties."

Joyce was a little embarrassed, but Joyce's mom told her since I didn't have a problem with the age difference that she should just get over it. I laughed.

A mixture of emotions came over me when it was time to leave Chicago. I was sad leaving my new extended family, yet I was excited about going back home. Elaine brought our little dog Pablo to the nursing home and I was excited to get him back with us. With our suitcases packed in the car, Pablo safely in his cage and Joyce behind the steering wheel, I climbed into my spot in the car and waved goodbye to everyone. We were on our way.

CHAPTER THIRTY EIGHT

ENEMA LADY WITH A HEART

H E'S NICE AND SO HANDSOME." "Yes, he is very loving and kind and I just adore him. I feel so loved and accepted by him. It feels so good to be with someone who is so loving. However, the age difference still bothers me and I am trying to work that out in my mind." "He doesn't seem to be bothered by the age difference, so you need to get over it." "I'm trying. I'm almost there." "Well, get there."

"Didn't you work next door when you were a teenager?" "Wow, that is a good memory. Yes, that is when I thought I wanted to be a nurse. The hospital was in the process of being built and I went through the nurse's aid program and ended up working on the medical floor. I was too small to work in orthopedics and too young to work in the nursery. I would have loved to work in the psychiatric ward, however, that floor had not yet been built." As mom and I continued to talk, my mind wandered back to that time.

"Since you are the new girl you get to feed the patient in 3A. Be careful; he has a terminal illness and can be very touchy." As I entered the patient's room, I was taken aback by his screaming, "It's about time you bring me food. You know I'm dying here." I remember apologizing and probably said something lame in response. I started to raise the back of his bed so he would be in a better position to receive his food, but as I did, he started yelling, "Hey, you can't be moving my bed. I'm in a lot of pain, and moving the bed makes it worse. I can eat my food lying down." "Oh my," I thought. "I am in trouble. I remember that no matter what I did or how I did it, he would yell at me. That was my first day at the hospital. He was my first patient and that was my initiation since I was the "new kid" on the block. I later learned that he was like that with everyone. He was a very cantankerous man. Obviously he was scared and in a lot of pain, so on some level, I couldn't blame him.

Our floor had thirty-two patients and I was charged with half. In the eighteen months I worked there we had at least twenty-nine terminally-ill patients at all times. During that time medical oncology did not exist as a clinical specialty. The main issue of that day was whether cancer drugs caused more harm than good and curing cancer with drugs didn't seem to be the mindset of that time. So, patients were made to feel more comfortable with pain medication and trial and error drugs.

I was drawn back into memories of some of the patients I spent time with. There was one lady who hallucinated about driving a big trailer truck. She would talk as if she were on one of those CBs and even had a handle. Her daughter said she always wanted to drive a big rig. I guess she was doing so in her delusions. Another patient, who was blind, would tell me stories of how she ended up with her current seeing-eye dog. Apparently she had a training dog that not only got her lost in the subway system of Chicago, but used to get sick on the moving train. She had to help the dog off the train and figure out where she was and how to get both of them home.

Then there was the patient that was under observation for nerves. I really didn't know what that meant, however, I found out one day when I walked into his room. I saw and said hello to his roommate who was sitting up watching television and the patient that was under observation was just lying on the bed. His eyes were open, so I approached him and asked if there was anything he needed or I might have asked him if he was alright. In either case, he jumped up out of his bed waving his hands and yelling. He had scared me when he jumped up so I jumped back and ran towards the door. He leaped and ran after me. I started yelling for a nurse as I stood there holding the door shut. It felt like an eternity holding that door while he was tugging on it from inside. Finally, several nurses and a doctor came running. They ended up restraining the patient. That man ultimately ended up breaking a nurse's nose when she tried to bathe him. He had been restrained but somehow managed to get his fist just at the right angle to sock her. No wonder he was under observation.

"Remember when I used to make you take off your uniform outside when you came home from work?"

"Yes, and even though I understood taking off my uniform, but I didn't understand why I had to take off my underwear as well. Standing just about naked outside in the cold was so uncomfortable."

"That was silly. I don't know what I was thinking. Well, you know your mother; sometimes I don't have a reason for why I do or did such things."

"Didn't you have to take care of the people who died? I think you told me that once."

"Yes. The first time I had to take care of someone who died, I was only seventeen years old. It was surreal. There I was preparing a "body" for the coroner. I felt like I didn't know what I was doing in spite of all my training. I was numb. As I stripped down the "body" I kept reminding myself that this was no longer a person. It always seemed that people would die on my shift and that was mostly in the evening or late night. In spite of how hard and sad that job could be I really liked it. I loved helping the patients. Giving enemas became my specialty and I was known by the patients as the "enema lady with a heart." That name stuck and all the patients who needed enemas asked for me."

"How did you end up with that name?"

"Well, when I gave an enema, even though the rule was you couldn't stop the flow of liquid until it was all gone, I would stop the flow if the patient was getting cramps or became uncomfortable in any way. The word got around and I became the "enema lady with a heart." "That's funny. If I need one I'll be sure to call you."

CHAPTER THIRTY-NINE

GIVE ME A SARSAPARILLA

A S WE PULLED OUT OF THE PARKING LOT I could tell that Joyce felt sad about leaving. "Your mom is really nice and pretty too." "Yes, she is!" "It's nice that you are so close; it's like you are best friends." "For the most part we have always been close. She has been a good friend. She sure likes you a lot." "I'm glad; I was a little worried about that."

I sat back and just enjoyed watching the different scenery all through Wisconsin. The scenery consisted of farms, cows, and more cows. I have never seen so many cows. Where I come from, there are no cows wandering around. I thought to myself, "Such a different world." I learned that Wisconsin is a dairy state where some of our cheese comes from. I love cheese. As we made our way through the state and into Minnesota, I was the motel locator. I learned how to read a map on our road trip, so I was able to find us a nice motel in a little town off the main road. After a nice dinner, we just crashed in our room to prepare for our next day.

Wow, when we entered South Dakota, the rugged landscape was so awesome. Joyce shared some of her experiences when camping in the Badlands when her son was a baby. She told me about the prairie dogs, the sod houses, and how fossils of prehistoric animals were found there. I learned so much and now know a little about the Badlands in South Dakota

Mt. Rushmore

Keystone, South Dakota

We continued on to a small Western town that had a famous historic drug store. It was unlike any drugstore that I have ever seen. It had started out small, grew and grew, and now is a tourist attraction. The sidewalks had poles with rings cemented into them near the curb. I learned that this was to tie up a horse. Even though there were bricked streets for cars in this little Western town, at one time everyone rode horses. It would have been an amazing time to be part of, although I feel that I am living during an amazing time and living an amazing life.

We walked around, took pictures, and had a sarsaparilla. Sarsaparilla, I learned, is a drink that some cowboys would order instead of whiskey at the saloons. These cowboys were usually made fun of because it was considered a soda pop.

"Do our stores sell sarsaparilla?"

"No, I don't think so. I think rootbeer is the closest drink to sarsaparilla."

We left that drug store and that little Western town and ventured on towards the mountain where the presidents' faces were carved.

"What is the name of that mountain that we are going to see?"

"Mount Rushmore."

We were back on the road again heading toward Mount Rushmore. I was so excited to see something in person that I only had seen in pictures. As we went winding through the mountain, I just looked from right to left. The hills were so beautiful. We took a cutoff, a small town popped up, and we headed for the motel where our reservation was. As we were checking in, the motel manager told us that there was no cable or television. He asked us if that was okay. He said that the cable had gone out and wouldn't be fixed for a couple of days. I guess our faces showed our disappointment with that news, however, we told him that it really did not matter to us, and then we just confirmed that our dog was welcome. They did not allow dogs to stay at their motel. The clerk that took our reservation was new and had given us the wrong information. The manager picked up the phone and made a call. When he was done, he sent us down the road to another motel. As it turned out, it was actually nicer. Everything turned out for the better. Everything was perfect!

The town was an old Western town nestled in the mountains. "How about a nice dinner?" "Yes, I sure could use some food. The last thing I had was that sarsaparilla and that didn't fill me up." "How about that

Keystone, South Dakota

Shawn and Joyce

Mitchell, South Dakata

place? It looks interesting. It is a steak place." We both laughed for each of us knew what the other was thinking. "This time we each get our own."

"Look at this. It is an old Western dance hall." "Is this where the ladies entertained the cowboys, like in the movies you watch?" "Yes, just like that." I had a wonderful dinner. The steak was perfect; both of ours were. Everything was perfect. We walked back to our motel hand-in-hand and I thought how grateful I was to be alive, a feeling that was foreign to me. That felt so good. What a perfect trip, a perfect dinner, a perfect night.

Driving up the windy mountain road I could see the carved faces from a distance due to the early morning sunlight shining on the mountain. As we got closer, I felt myself getting more and more excited, and suddenly I was standing right in front of the faces of four of our country's most famous presidents. They were much bigger than I thought they would be. I felt so privileged being there. "How did this get carved?" "Well, here is a plaque with some information on it. Let's see."

"It says here, "A man named Gutzon Borglum and his son Lincoln were the carvers and it took fourteen years to complete the four presidents: George Washington, Thomas Jefferson, Theodore Roosevelt and Abraham Lincoln." "They had skills." "They sure did." "I love looking at them. Why don't we eat lunch on the outside patio?" "Okay." As I sat eating my hamburger I just stared in amazement at the faces carved into the side of a mountain. Who would have thought a kid from the projects, growing up in an orphanage and group homes would be sitting in a café at Mt. Rushmore? I was overwhelmed with such a feeling of gratitude. I could have sat there all day and we almost did.

Several hours later we were driving back down the mountain road to a national park. "There, look, buffalo. Actual buffalo." I couldn't believe I was seeing buffalo just roaming around. We were so close I could almost touch them. "I didn't know they were so big." "Yes, they are big aren't they?" As we left the park, my head turned from side to side trying to get one last look at the buffalo. "That was thrilling for me to see."

Driving the back roads of the West was so beautiful and exciting. There were horses running alongside us with mountains in the distance as their backdrop. "Do those horses belong to anyone?" "Yes, this land is all private ranches." The hours of that day seemed to pass so quickly and it was starting to get dark. I began my motel search. There were not too many where we were. I did find one and we decided to stop since it had been a very long day.

We pulled into the parking lot of a discount motel and I immediately became very fearful. A couple of guys were barbecuing outside one of the rooms and I realized they were living in the motel. Joyce checked us in and our room turned out to be a couple of doors down from this family. As we were unloading the car, one of the young men yelled out to a woman, who I assume was his mom. "I don't want to be around any nigger." A loud voice responded ,"Be quiet I don't want to be kicked out. I need to live here." "Well, now I was afraid."

We stopped unloading the car and decided that it would be best to keep our things in the car instead of the room. I was worried about my shoes. I actually obsess about my shoes. I had taken five pairs of shoes with me and didn't want them stolen. These were punks. I was not sure if they were thugs or not. While we were deciding we walked over to the little restaurant that was attached to the parking lot and had a quick bite to eat. When we came back, I went over and started talking to them and that took the edge off of the situation. I was still cautious, but less afraid. We decided to continue to unpack the car. By the time we were finished, we were both so tired that we just fell into bed and passed out.

CHAPTER FORTY

PLANNING

A N ARTIST'S PALETTE OF COLORS lay before me as I drove our last leg of the trip through the mountains of Colorado and New Mexico. The beauty of all the colors blending together brought to mind all the wonderful drawings that Shawn had created while he was in prison. He would send them to me as he did them. I saved them all. Those thoughts started me thinking about getting married to Shawn. When Shawn asked me to marry him, at first, I didn't take him seriously. Then I realized he was very serious. We fell in love and getting married was the next logical step for him and now for me, too.

"It's like a kaleidoscope; the colors change the farther we drive," said Shawn.

"You're right. All the colors reminded me of the drawings you did. You are really good and I hope you continue to draw."

"I love to draw, however, I used to do it to cope. I have kind of lost interest in it."

A town in Arizona was our evening stop. What a change from the night before. Our room was like a suite. The bed was huge. After a nice dinner, we just settled in knowing that we would be back home the next day.

"Boy, I will be glad to get home."

"Me too, then we can get married."

"Shawn, are you really sure?"

"Yes, I love you and I am in love with you."

"So, I have to ask you one more time, what about the age difference?"

"That is not an issue for me. Your age turns me on, and besides you don't even look your age." "Thanks, you always make me feel so good. Okay then, how do you want our wedding to look?" "Can we get married on the beach?"

"I think that would be lovely. What do you want to wear?"

"I want to wear white, like a white jacket and white pants."

"Okay. What color should I wear?"

"Maybe a black dress, then we would be in black and white."

"Shawn, that's cool. It will be black and white in reverse. So, when we get back, I think the first thing we need to do is get you fitted for a tuxedo."

"Wow, I actually get a tuxedo?"

"Of course, and I will start looking for a dress right away."

"I am so excited! Getting married in a white tux, wow!"

My thoughts were all over the place as I continued driving home where my new life would begin. Well, I guess it sort of already has begun. Getting married just didn't seem tangible. I looked over at Shawn and he had dozed off. I thought, "He is so loving and precious and being handsome just is a bonus." I always feel good around him. He emits such great energy, so positive. It was amazing to me since I know he deals with a lot due to his mental illness. I wondered if he would have to deal with the voices in his head for the rest of his life, or if they would subside or completely go away in time. He is and will continue to be in a safe, stable, loving environment, maybe for the first time in his life, and maybe, just maybe his mind would heal. If it were in my power I would love to give that to him as a wedding gift. So my gift will be a silent prayer for that healing.

I drove home in serene bliss. I felt so happy and content. The desert terrain in all its blooming flora paved my way as I drove toward the busyness of the city. They seemed to be forming little bouquets all around me. It was such a validating sign that I was making the right decision in marrying Shawn. In spite of all of our differences, the decision just felt right!

CHAPTER 41

"WHAT? TAKE OFF MY PANTS?"

S O, WHY ARE YOU FOLKS HERE?"

"We're getting married and need a tuxedo. Can I get a white one?"

"Yes, we can arrange that. We'll need to take measurements so come on back with me and we will take care of that."

There I was, trying on different jackets to get the right size. I really didn't realize how big I had gotten from all the exercise, for it took a while to find the right fit. My waist and legs were measured and it felt really funny to me. My shyness coupled with my anxiety started to kick in and I just wished they had a tuxedo that I could just put on and leave. Not the case. Measurements, measurements, and more measurements.

"I get white shoes too?" I asked the tailor.

"Yes, and a white shirt and tie as well."

"This is so cool."

"We'll have it ready for you in a couple of days."

Those were a long couple of days for me since I couldn't wait to put that tuxedo on. What a trip. Me, in a tuxedo!

"Mr. Hall, your tuxedo is ready in the back. We'll just have you take off your clothes and you can try it on."

"What, take off my pants? I'm sure it will fit just fine."

"Well, we will have to try the tuxedo pants on to make sure the waist and the leg length are right. You can go into the dressing room and try the pants on."

"Alright."

Boy, I sure was feeling anxious, for I have never really had to do anything like this before. So, I reluctantly walked back into the dressing room, took off my clothes, including my pants, and first put on the white pants, then the shirt and then the jacket. I didn't know how to tie the tie so I left it off. When I walked out everyone looked at me and just said "Wow!" I blushed however, when I looked in the mirror. I just said, "Damn, I look good." If no one had been around, I would have just stood in front of that mirror all day. I sure looked good. I wanted to yell, "I'm stylin'." Man, I looked good. If my family could see me now.

CHAPTER FORTY-TWO

THE MANNEQUIN THAT SAVED THE DAY

WHY IS IT SO HARD TO FIND A SIMPLE BLACK DRESS? I have looked and looked and looked. Either they are way too fancy or too short or too low or just too something. I must have said, "I am looking for a simple black dress," at least twenty times. I said it to every salesperson who approached me in the different stores I walked into.

All of a sudden, I was just about to give up and leave when I saw someone putting a long black dress on a naked mannequin in the back of the store.

"Wait a minute," I said to the lady dressing the mannequin. "I am looking for that exact dress. Where are more like that one?"

"This is the only one we have."

"What size is it?"

"Medium."

"I'll take it."

I didn't even have to try it on since I knew it would fit. Everything was coming together by divine providence.

I was so excited about getting married to Shawn and I couldn't believe my own excitement. This feeling was a new one for me, for I never felt like this when I married my late husband. I loved him, but was never really in love with him. This is a first for me and I am just wallowing in this feeling.

"Shawn, should we get Tiki torches?"

"Yes, that would be cool. Fire on the beach."

"So we have everything that we need so far, your wedding outfit and my dress, the minister, the place, the day and the time, however, what about our vows? Should we write our own?"

"I want to play you a song as my vows."

"Oh, that will be nice. Well, then I'll play a song for you as well."

I don't think there were two more excited people in the world. Neither one of us could talk about our wedding without getting choked up. We asked my daughter to be part of the wedding ceremony and our friend, the one who knew I was in love with Shawn before I knew it. She wanted to get my bouquet and I thought that was the nicest offer since I hadn't even thought about getting a bouquet. How special! We were now ready for our big day.

CHAPTER FORTY-THREE

PROVIDENCE

OUR DAY HAD COME.

"Shawn, my insides are just jumping up and down. I feel like I am in my own personal fairy tale and you brought me my glass slipper."

"Hey, it's our fairy tale, and yes, I brought you the glass slipper in the form of my heart."

"Aw, so romantic."

"Oh, what a beautiful bouquet of red roses. I love them."

"I got everyone a red rose to wear."

"Thank you."

Joyce's daughter said, "Mom, you look so pretty, let's take some pictures before we get to the beach. Stand over there by the tree. Nice. Both of you look so much in love."

"We are."

We were driven to the beach, and met the minister and her husband in the lobby of a very exclusive hotel. They had non-alcoholic drinks in Champagne glasses waiting for all of us. The minister gave us a toast, and posed us for pictures. I felt like a queen and I am quite sure that Shawn felt like a king. We were the celebrities of the hotel.

The minister and her husband led the way with my daughter and our friend close behind. Shawn and I followed behind this mini procession. We weaved our way down a path until we reached a sand clearing between two dunes. The minister and her husband put the Tiki torches in the sand and lit them. We had brought a portable recorder to play our vows which the minister's husband was in charge and my daughter and our friend took their place beside each one of us.

The view of the ocean behind the minister was breathtaking. The sun was getting ready to set so the sky was a mixture of beautiful blues and oranges. We were definitely in paradise.

The ceremony began with a prayer, which led into the normal dialog for a wedding. I was holding onto Shawn's arm so tightly that I am sure he was bruised the next day. We kept looking at each other with eyes that spoke of our love for each other. It was magical.

When it came time for vows, the minister played *I Met a Little Girl* by Marvin Gaye which was Shawn's vows. The words were very meaningful to me. They spoke of his feelings for me and how and when he decided he wanted to marry me. I held on to his arm like we were going to be blown away by some great wind and looked into his eyes while the words were filling my heart. Tears of joy filled my eyes and I wanted to hang on to this moment forever.

Now time for my vows to Shawn. The minister's husband pushed the play button and the words poured out from the little speaker. I chose the song *I Will Love You Forever* by Pollyanna; the title really said it all. I knew that I would love Shawn forever.

The minister put together a beautiful ceremony to include readings from the book *The Little Prince* by Antoine de Saint-Exupery, a ring exchange and inspirational words designed uniquely for us. When asked that famous question that begins with "Do you... We both answered, "I do." "I do."

This is it. The missing piece to my life's puzzle. My puzzle is now complete.

CHAPTER FORTY-FOUR

TO BE
CONTINUED

I T HAS BEEN OVER TWO YEARS since our marriage ceremony and our journey still continues. We have had our ups and downs however overcoming each challenge has deepened our relationship.

The following pictures are of some of our travels and experiences these past two years.

Disneyland

Near Gallup, New Mexico

Yellowstone National Park

Route 66

Grand Canyon Skywalk

Hualapai Ranch

Bagdad Café

Hualapai Ranch

Hualapai Reservation, West Rim,
Grand Canyon

Disneyland

Vow renewal ceremony

Joyce's birthday celebration

Cracker Barrel

Karate champion   *Karate champion*

Los Angeles Art Show